Internal Communication and Employer Brands

This book proposes a model of internal communication based on empirical research to demonstrate how contemporary organizations strategize, organize, perform, and measure it.

Internal communication is the management of communication between an organization and its members to inform, motivate, engage, and cocreate meanings to make organizations more effective. The book presents key concepts defining the successful implementation and execution of internal communication: internal communication satisfaction, employee engagement, employer branding, organizational support, and psychological contract fulfillment. Including an extensive literature review and informed by in-depth interviews conducted with corporate communication directors and human resource management directors in 25 Croatian organizations, the book uses original research to give practical guidance on internal communication best practices.

The book is an ideal resource for researchers and advanced students of public relations and corporate communication broadly and internal and employee communication specifically.

Ana Tkalac Verčič is a professor at the Faculty of Economics & Business at the University of Zagreb. Her research includes various communication topics, mostly in internal communication. She has published more than 100 papers and chapters and has authored and edited numerous books in public relations and marketing.

Dejan Verčič is a professor and Head of the Centre for Marketing and Public Relations at the Faculty of Social Sciences, University of Ljubljana, and Partner and Knowledge Director at Herman & partnerji d.o.o., Slovenia. His research interests are globalization, mediatization, reflective and strategic communication, and future studies.

Anja Špoljarić is a research assistant at the Faculty of Economics and Business, University of Zagreb. She is currently pursuing a PhD. Her doctoral thesis will explore the relationship between internal communication and employer brands. Her research and published articles deal with communication, specifically internal communication and employer branding.

Routledge Research in Public Relations

Bringing together theories and thought from a variety of perspectives, this series features cutting-edge research addressing all the major issues in public relations today, helping to define and advance the field.

4 **The Bauhaus and Public Relations**
Communication in a Permanent State of Crisis
Patrick Rössler

5 **Public Relations and Religion in American History**
Evangelism, Temperance, and Business
Margot Opdycke Lamme

6 **Public Relations in the Nonprofit Sector**
Theory and Practice
Edited by Richard D. Waters

7 **Public Relations and the Public Interest**
Jane Johnston

8 **The Moral Compass of Public Relations**
Edited by Brigitta R. Brunner

9 **Relationship Building in Public Relations**
Petra Theunissen and Helen Sissons

10 **Advancing Crisis Communication Effectiveness**
Integrating Public Relations Scholarship with Practice
Edited by Yan Jin, Bryan H. Reber, and Glen J. Nowak

11 **Internal Communication and Employer Brands**
Ana Tkalac Verčič, Dejan Verčič, and Anja Špoljarić

For more information about this series, please visit: https://www.routledge.com/Routledge-Research-in-Public-Relations/book-series/RRPR

"This is a welcome review of recent research and current thinking related to internal communication in organizations. Experience through the COVID pandemic has re-emphasized the importance of good, well thought through and managed internal communication and this new book will make a valuable contribution to this developing area of management practice."

Dr. Jon White, *Visiting Professor, Henley Business School, University of Reading, UK*

"Internal communication is more important than ever for all kinds of organizations. This timely book provides a comprehensive overview. It is an essential reading for leaders in human resources, communications, and general management."

Ansgar Zerfass, *Professor and Chair for Strategic Communication, Leipzig University, Germany*

"This book fills a key vacuum in the body of knowledge on the vital, albeit ignored, topic of internal communication. The authors are to be commended for conceptualizing a holistic approach to the concept while also presenting information of value both to academics and practitioners."

Dr. Krishnamurthy Sriramesh, *PhD, Professor of Public Relations, University of Colorado, Boulder, USA*

Internal Communication and Employer Brands

Ana Tkalac Verčič, Dejan Verčič, and Anja Špoljarić

Routledge
Taylor & Francis Group
NEW YORK AND LONDON

First published 2023
by Routledge
605 Third Avenue, New York, NY 10158

and by Routledge
4 Park Square, Milton Park, Abingdon, Oxon, OX14 4RN

Routledge is an imprint of the Taylor & Francis Group, an informa business

Library of Congress Cataloging-in-Publication Data
A catalog record for this title has been requested

ISBN: 978-1-032-05680-7 (hbk)
ISBN: 978-1-032-05978-5 (pbk)
ISBN: 978-1-003-20010-9 (ebk)

DOI: 10.4324/9781003200109

Typeset in Times New Roman
by KnowledgeWorks Global Ltd.

Contents

Acknowledgment

This work has been fully supported by the Croatian Science Foundation under project no. 3323.

1 What is internal communication?

The recent pandemic has amplified the importance of effective internal communication within organizations and corporations. Since before the pandemic, the rapid digitalization of business processes and transactions with customers has had far-reaching effects on communications within organizations, becoming a defining characteristic of the 21st century. Internal communication has historically been viewed quite simply as providing employees with information (McKenzie, 2007). Decades of research have demonstrated that, in fact, it affects all aspects of organizational performance (Men & Bowen, 2017; Tkalac Verčič et al., 2012), especially as organizations are increasingly connected, transparent, and digitized, and where employees are not only organizational insiders but also reliable sources of information to external audiences. In this context, the present work – and the research project behind it – describes empirical research aimed at understanding what makes internal communication difficult and what can help mitigate or prevent such barriers.

Theoretical positioning

The complexity of organizations means that they engage in communication across all levels, from between individuals to between one individual and the masses. This range of levels explains why various subdomains of communication and social sciences are dedicated to understanding communication in organizations (Jones et al., 2004), such as organizational psychology, organizational sociology, journalism, and speech communication (Grunig, 1992). In writing this book, we wish to clarify at the outset where we believe internal communication fits among the disciplines that often claim it, which include business, management, corporate, and organizational communication.

Internal communication has been variously referred to as integrated internal communications, internal public relations, employee communications, business communications, employee relations, internal relations, internal marketing, intra-organizational communication, and staff

DOI: 10.4324/9781003200109-1

communication (Lee & Yue, 2020; Men & Bowen, 2017; Tkalac Verčič et al., 2012). It has been explored within organizational and managerial theories (Thompkins, 1987), organizational communication (Goldhaber, 1993; Jablin et al., 1987; Jablin & Putnam, 2001), organizational psychology (Drenth et al., 1998; Lowenberg & Conrad, 1998), and public relations (Men & Bowen, 2017; Ruck & Welch, 2012; Tkalac Verčič et al., 2012; Welch, 2012). These various disciplines examine the interface between communication and organizational life (Miller, 1996) from quite different perspectives (Kalla, 2005). Nevertheless, even though internal communication is recognized as a crucial topic (Zerfass et al., 2010) and research on it has grown exponentially since 2011 (Lee & Yue, 2020), we believe the field of public relations has yet to take internal communication properly into account.

In 1992, Grunig reviewed theories of internal communication in the field of "organizational communication", which he considered the standard term used in academic departments of speech communication (p. 531), and he remarked that the field of speech communication had for many years an "almost exclusive privilege of colonizing the oasis of organizational communication" (p. 537) for lack of interest from academics in other fields. Grunig and others use the terms "organizational communication" and "internal communication" interchangeably (Quirke, 2008; Tourish & Hargie, 2009; Zwijze-Koning & de Jong, 2007), even though this can set up an "unhelpful continuous loop" in which authors having no alternatives define internal communication based on an outdated, transactional definition of organizational communication (Welch & Jackson, 2007).

We see internal communication as an integral part of public relations. The disciplines of public relations and organizational communication have different roots: public relations emerged from mass communication, while organizational communication originated in speech and interpersonal communication (Wehmeier & Winkler, 2013). Additionally, academics usually approach public relations as an organizational, managerial function that focuses on the relationship between the organization and its various audiences. In line with this approach, we study internal communication from a rationalist mindset as a strategic planning process. Like research in public relations, studies in internal communication emphasize quantitative, deductive analyses that can lead to generalizations applicable to specific managerial problems (Bessonov, 2008).

Organizational positioning

Within organizations, internal communication may occupy various positions within the organizational structure. In fact, organizations are often confused about which department or division should "own" internal communication (Helsby, 2002). For example, the departments of human resources and marketing may both claim internal communication as within their remit, yet it is usually the departments of public relations and corporate communication that best understand internal audiences (Tkalac Verčič, 2016). The position of internal communication in the organizational structure depends on the organization's size, culture, expectations, management style, financial resources, and employee characteristics (Tkalac Verčič, 2021).

When we began the project from which this book emerged, we wanted to test the possibility that internal communication might be part of a wider, internal marketing concept, since internal marketing covers all contacts with internal stakeholders (Sinčić Ćorić & Pološki Vokić, 2009). After surveying 26 corporations in Croatia, we found this rarely to be the case. Instead, our study confirmed Helsby's (2002) conclusion that internal communication is located mostly in communication departments. We also found, as Grunig (1992) mentioned 30 years ago, that "most organizations have some program of internal communication" (Grunig, 1992, p. 533). In fact, as he reported, all the organizations in our sample had communication programs involving a publication and other forms of mediated communication.

What has indeed changed in the last decade is that internal communication has become formalized as an explicit responsibility, more often of a person than a department, under which all forms of employee communication are managed. Even so, some confusion remains among top management about the position that internal communication should occupy in the organization. Occasionally, it is perceived only as a messaging function. Others, in contrast, may see it as a key change agent that can help organizations confront various issues (Helsby, 2002; Tkalac Verčič, 2021). Our work (Tkalac Verčič et al., 2012) has shown that internal communication managers usually report to the human resource manager, corporate communications manager, or directly to the CEO. Nevertheless, "few if any directors of internal communication [sit] alongside the other directors in the boardroom" (Smith & Mounter, 2008, p. 15). Confirming our previous results (Tkalac Verčič et al., 2012), the research project giving rise to the present book found that internal communication should be a part of corporate communication departments, positioned relatively high in the organizational structure, in order to ensure the best results. More on this can be found in Chapter 2.

Communication channels

In exploring the scope of internal communication, we considered contemporary communication channels, as we detail in Chapter 4. Channels can range from traditional print publications such as newsletters to telephone calls and face-to-face communication, all the way to interactive web tools such as internal social networking sites (Crescenzo, 2011). Each medium involves a different kind of engagement as well as different communication scales and speeds. We found that research on internal communication channels is sorely lacking, especially given that new communication technologies are completely reshaping our world. Early research on communication channels was limited to upward, downward, and horizontal flows of information through the organization, and it conceptualized communication mainly as the dissemination of information (Grunig, 1992), leading to a focus on such topics as information overload and types of distortion in the channels.

Media richness theory is among the frameworks most often used to evaluate and compare the effectiveness of different communication channels (Daft & Lengel, 1984, 1986). The theory focuses on the richness of a medium, defined as the ability to enable users to communicate and to ensure understanding and eliminate equivocality of the task involved. Rich media are often the most appropriate for effective, symmetrical internal communication (Men, 2014). Although formulated nearly 40 years ago, media richness theory is proving useful for examining communication channels even with today's massive shift toward digital technologies (Tkalac Verčič & Špoljarić, 2020).

Corporate adoption of new technologies is not straightforward (Tkalac Verčič & Špoljarić, 2020). Even as digitalization in the workplace is becoming the norm, whether employees embrace it is another question. Friedl and Tkalac Verčič (2011) showed that not all employees younger than 30 years are completely immersed in digital technology. McKinsey Global Institute (2016) conducted an online survey of 2,427 employees across the full range of regions, industries, company sizes, functional specialties, and tenures. Over two-thirds of the respondents believed that social technologies could increase the quality of internal communication. Numerous studies have pointed out that, from the perspective of public relations, social media – which includes everything from social networks to blogs – benefits organizations by building internal communities (Men & Bowen, 2017), enhancing perceived transparency (Men et al., 2020), helping engage employees (Sievert & Scholz, 2017), increasing interaction, and strengthening employee engagement (Crescenzo, 2011). By creating dialogue, social media can strongly influence traditional media (Berger, 2008; Lee, 2018). They can also promote listening skills and face-to-face communication (Rhee, 2004). At the same time, further research is needed to examine to what extent computer-mediated communication meets employees' professional and personal needs (Braun et al., 2019).

The project giving rise to the present book makes clear that when choosing employee communication channels, organizations should take into account the preferences of their employees. Even though positive attitudes toward media are a prerequisite for successful internal communication (Welch, 2012), organizations usually choose communication channels based not on employee preferences but numerous other factors, such as the organization's size, profile, culture, external environment, and employees' qualifications (Dévényi, 2016). Aligning internal communication with employee preferences and perceptions is the only option if organizations wish to be successful in the future. Gone are the days when organizations could simply expect employees to adapt to their communication channels. The first step can involve simply asking employees what they think and how they feel about internal communication practices. Of course, organizations also need to keep up with changing trends in communication tools, but only tools that align with employee preferences are likely to be successful in the long term.

Research and evaluation of internal communication in this book

Within this project, we approach internal communication as an organizational function that involves different strategies and tactics, which can be managed well only if they are continuously and carefully evaluated. We detail the types of measurement at length in Chapter 5, so here we want to focus only on what we measured and why. Our research began from the assumption that communication in organizations is rarely treated as an activity in its own right, as something beyond mere dissemination of information, and therefore that it tends to be monitored intuitively. More systematic assessment of internal communication, in contrast, can offer managers a clear, comprehensive picture of what the situation in the organization really is, which reduces the natural managerial tendency toward "self-aggrandizement" and can bypass the common problem of employee reluctance to provide honest feedback (Tourish & Hargie, 2009). Indeed, as Hargie and Tourish (2009) note, incomplete assessment of internal communications leads many organizations to repeat well-worn mistakes even as they realize the need for improvement. Through continuous evaluation, in contrast, an organization can improve communication because it can assess the baseline and the degree of potential improvement.

Traditionally, communication within organizations has been viewed as a linear process, in which the message is transmitted from the sender to the receiver (Goldhaber et al., 1978). Analysis of communication has therefore focused on how this process can be managed and improved (Tourish & Hargie, 2009). More recently, research has moved toward conceptualizing communication as a set of processes embedded within larger organizational systems (Mumby, 2007). In the current approach to organizational communication, the focus is on the construction of meaning among organizational actors, who influence one another (Tourish, 2007). Within the context of public relations, internal communication has grown rapidly as a discipline, and its analysis has focused on a different set of approaches than organizational communication. Topics of research have included employee behaviors, such as employee opinion, dissent, communicative behaviors, and organizational citizenship.

Research has also begun to focus on outcomes for employees and the organization, such as job satisfaction, engagement, organizational identification, employee voice, and advocacy (Lee & Yue, 2020).

Assessments of everyday internal communication practices, which often take the form of "communication audits", typically measure employee attitudes toward communication. Such assessments, which we define in Chapter 5, evaluate communication interactions and how the participants perceive them. Our project established that internal communication professionals do not know enough about communication audits or, more generally, how to assess communication practices. This highlights the need for academia to take the lead in developing a body of knowledge that can guide practitioners.

We believe that communication audits and, more generally, the evaluation of internal communication should fulfill the following five principles (Tkalac Verčič & Verčič, 2005). First, internal communication audits should analyze cognitive, emotional, and behavioral components of organizational life at the level of the individual, group, organization or society, depending on the initial definition of the problem. Second, internal communication audits should take into account all populations that can be identified as stakeholders, namely those who affect organizations and/or are affected by them, as well as society at large as the carrier of culture and legitimacy. Third, individuals, groups, organizations, and society need to be conceptualized in accordance with contemporary perspectives, and any simplifications should be explicitly justified. Fourth, any potential conflicts between the pursuit of scientific rigor (high reliability and validity) and the pursuit of practical usefulness should be explicitly addressed. Fifth, internal communication audits need to be seen as an interdisciplinary project.

Consequences of good internal communication

Like research in public relations, research in internal communication should evolve with changing practices in order to address issues relevant to organizations. These topics cover a range of managerial issues, including crisis management, employee behaviors, internal media, employee engagement, leadership, and ethics (Lee & Yue, 2020). Another important research area is employee perceptions of internal communication and their attitudes toward their work, since those attitudes influence work outcomes at the levels of the individual and organization (Carrière & Bourque, 2009). For such research, we have found social exchange theory to be quite useful (Cropanzano et al., 2017). Social exchange theory conceptualizes communication processes as reciprocal resource exchanges, and such exchanges within organizations can foster prosocial attitudes and behaviors (Einwiller et al., 2021) and stabilize good relationships (Cropanzano & Mitchell, 2005). In theory, successful reciprocal exchanges between employer and employee can transform something that might seem a purely economic relationship into a high-quality social connection.

In our project, we followed the assumptions of social exchange theory to approach internal communication as the initiator of social exchange between employer and employee. In other words, we contend that a high-quality social exchange in an organization starts with timely, informative internal communication. Therefore, we expect that a higher level of internal communication satisfaction will lead employees to perceive their relationship with their employer more favorably. We used two organizational behavior constructs, perceived organizational support (Eisenberger et al., 2020) and psychological contract fulfillment (Coyle-Shapiro et al., 2019), to assess the beliefs and feelings that employees have about their relationship with their employer. We hypothesized that employees' satisfaction with internal communication would correlate with their assessments of the quality of their social exchanges with their employer. We further hypothesized, based on previous work by us (Tkalac Verčič et al., 2021) and others (Mishra et al., 2014; Pugh & Dietz, 2008; Tkalac Verčič & Pološki Vokić, 2017; Welch, 2011; Wiley et al., 2010), that employees' perception of a higher quality relationship with their employer would translate to greater engagement and stronger perception of employer attractiveness. In our project, we applied well-defined indicators of social exchange quality, as detailed in Chapter 9.

Branding, a well-developed concept in marketing, can also apply to employees, in which case it refers to the sum of organizational efforts to communicate to employees, current and potential, that it is a desirable place to work (Lloyd, 2002). This dimension of branding, which is increasingly becoming the responsibility of corporate communications within the organization, is in early stages of research (Backhaus & Tikoo, 2004). Such branding is supported by appropriate external and internal communication (Prasad, 2019). In our project, we explored engagement and employer brands in Chapters 7 and 8. We found that psychological contract agreement and perceived organizational support mediated the relationship between internal communication satisfaction on one hand and engagement and employer attractiveness on the other. These results show how internal communication can influence work-related outcomes, for which a clear understanding of the organizational context is essential.

In a world where organizational transformation is the norm, achieving psychological contract agreement and organizational support is not always easy. Therefore, managers of corporate communications and internal communications should understand how these two variables influence employee behavior and attitudes toward the organization. Organizations should ensure that all their internal communication procedures are effective, with clear, two-way communication that highlights mutual obligations. Sufficiently open communication can foster a stronger employee perception of organizational support and intensify the psychological contract (Argenti, 1998). As a result, employees will feel engaged and consider their employees attractive (Tkalac Verčič et al., 2021).

Change, trust, and organizational culture

Successful organizational change, whether it involves downsizing, crises, mergers, acquisitions, or adoption of new technology, requires appropriate communication (Goodman & Truss, 2004; Kotter, 1996), including effective internal communication (Kitchen & Daly, 2002). Whether trying to maintain the *status quo* or trying to grow, managers need to understand what drives change and how to achieve it. Communication can support organizational change by reducing uncertainty and resistance to change, while facilitating employee participation, shared understanding, and mutual engagement (Men & Bowen, 2017). By including employees in the change process, internal communication can help them understand the change and its impact (Goodman & Truss, 2004), which in turn can make the difference between whether the change succeeds or fails (Henderson & McAdam, 2003).

Despite the importance of effective communication for successful change (Proctor & Doukakis, 2003; Young & Post, 1993), how managers should communicate during change is not well understood. While it seems clear that communication should be context-specific (Balogun & Hope-Hailey, 2003), selecting the appropriate content and channels is challenging (Goodman & Truss, 2004).

Internal communication is important for creating and maintaining trust within organizations undergoing change processes (Botan & Taylor, 2004; Mayer & Gavin, 2005). Trust between employees and managers can be built through communication that is open (Mishra & Mishra, 1994) as well as appropriate, clear, and timely (Chia, 2005). Organizations can benefit by building trust with their employees through good internal communication because the latter feel engaged and empowered to build better customer relationships(Mishra & Boynton, 2011). Internal communication should take into account the diverse dimensions of trust in order to foster it (Röttger & Voß, 2008).

In this way, internal communication must be considered within the social-organizational context in which it operates, which has led to research into how such communication shapes organizational culture and is, in turn, shaped by it. Organizational culture influences organizational effectiveness (Šimanskienė, 2002) and determines various aspects of organizational life (Berger, 2008). This conception of culture requires something broader than the typical conception in public relations, which has focused on the culture of the individuals in the society in which the organization operates, and less on the intra-organizational culture (Rhee & Moon, 2009). The culture within an organization can be analyzed in terms of the communication among employees (Men & Bowen, 2017; Men & Yue, 2019). By integrating, rather than ignoring, the multiple sources of culture among its employees, an organization can build an inclusive, consensual culture (Pinnington, 2003). Research is urgently needed to identify how internal communication can contribute to that culture creation.

Defining internal communication and the research model in the present project

Internal communication is hugely important and yet taken for granted, which the global COVID-19 pandemic has made all too clear as organizations have rushed to enable remote working and struggled to deal with the internal communication challenges that come with it. During the pandemic, purposeful internal communication has been essential in providing essential health information to employees and serving as the "glue" holding them together.

Our research project has shown that even a marginal increase in effort to manage internal communication can bring sizeable increases in employee satisfaction with internal communication. The digitization of communication has brought challenges. To help organizations deal with this and myriad other challenges, we launched our project to explore the scope and practice of internal communication and offer a theoretical definition that reflects the reality of practice. We approached internal communication mainly from a public relations point of view, beginning with the idea that internal communication means managing relationships with internal audiences. In trying to shape an overall definition that reflects our new digital reality, we considered the general approaches such as "sharing information in an organization" and "all communication within an organization". We also considered some definitions established by public relations scholars.

In previous studies, we proposed that internal communication creates and maintains communication systems between employers and employees (Tkalac Verčič, 2019). Bahtijarević-Šiber and Sikavica (2001) defined communication in organizations as an exchange of information, ideas, attitudes, and emotions from one person to another, with the common goal of changing behavior. Kalla (2005) defined internal communication "as integrated internal communication, i.e., all formal and informal communication taking place internally at all levels of an organization" (2005, p. 304), while Welch and Jackson (2007) defined it as "the strategic management of interactions and relationships between stakeholders within organizations" and specific interrelated dimensions that include "internal line manager communication, internal team peer communication, internal project peer communication and internal corporate communication" (p. 184). Men and Bowen (2017) described it as "the strategic management of internal communication in managing interdependence and building mutually beneficial relationships between the organization and its employees" (p. 12). We relied on all these definitions in our attempt to determine what internal communication is today.

We argue in Chapter 3 that internal communication is an integral part of management, serving various purposes from informing and persuading to negotiating and creating meaning. Internal communication must be seen as part of strategic management because of its importance to organizational outcomes. One of the goals of our project was to reframe the definition of internal communication to make it more authentic to what occurs within organizations. After careful consideration, we propose the following definition:

> Internal communication is the management of communication between an organization and its members to inform, motivate, engage, and co-create meaning in order to make organizations more effective.

In addition, our project aimed to connect this conceptualization of internal communication with employee engagement and employer brands through psychological contract fulfillment, perceived organizational support, and other mediating variables (Figure 1.1). This book lays out our process and findings in the next chapters.

The main objective of this book is to widen the scope of defining internal communication and adjust the starting definition so that it accurately reflects internal communication in its organizational context. Another objective is to determine the most common organizational position of internal communication in organizations and to determine whether this position reflects what corporate communication directors and human resource directors consider optimal. As part of these considerations, the book analyzes internal communication channels, paying special attention to internal publics' characteristics, segmentation approaches, social media, employee engagement, change management, leadership communication, and approaches to measurement and evaluation. Measuring

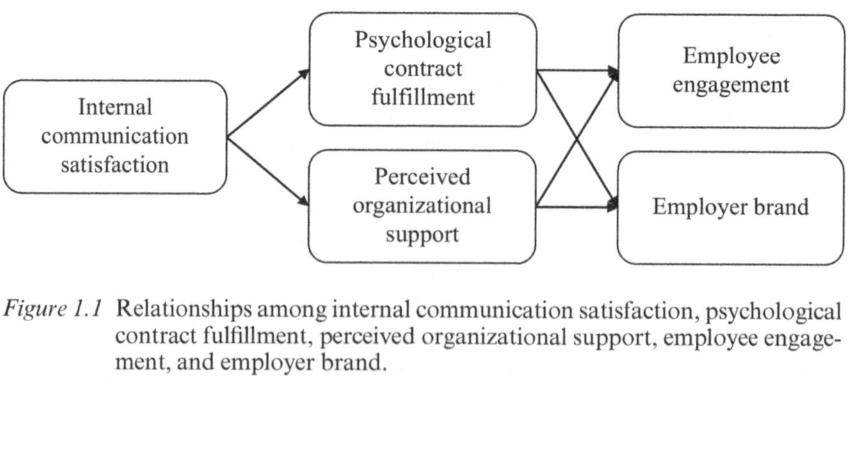

Figure 1.1 Relationships among internal communication satisfaction, psychological contract fulfillment, perceived organizational support, employee engagement, and employer brand.

the success of internal communication is possible through measurement of the retention of key organizational messages and through communication audits, co-orientational analyses, communication network analyses, and measurement of internal communication satisfaction. Thus, this book examines which methods are conducted in organizations, how often, and how successfully, and it explores how much the results are used to shape communication strategies. The book also links the analysis of internal communication satisfaction with measures of organizational success. Conducting internal communication with clear, well-defined goals leads to measurable results. Thus, in the end, the book aims to broaden theoretical and practical knowledge about the importance and role of internal communication in organizational success, which may help improve the corporate bottom line.

References

Argenti, P. A. (1998). Strategic employee communication. *Human Resource Management*, *37*(3/4), 199–206. https://doi.org/10.1002/(SICI)1099-050X(199823/24)37:3/4<199::AID-HRM3>3.0.CO;2-R

Backhaus, K., & Tikoo, S. (2004). Conceptualizing and researching employer branding. *Career Development International*, *9*(5), 501–517. https://doi.org/10.1108/13620430410550754

Bahtijarević-Šiber, F., & Sikavica, P. (2001). *Leksikon menedžmenta* [Management lexicon]. Masmedia.

Balogun, J., & Hope-Hailey, V. (2003). *Exploring strategic change* (2nd ed.). Prentice-Hall.

Berger, B. (2008, November 17). *Employee/organizational communications*. Institute for Public Relations. https://instituteforpr.org/employee-organizational-communications/

Bessonov, A. B. (2008). Communication processes: Role, place, content. *Scientific and Technical Information Processing*, *35*(4), 159–171. https://doi.org/10.3103/S0147688208040011

Botan, C. H., & Taylor, M. (2004). Public relations: State of the field. *Journal of Communication*, *54*(4), 645–661. https://doi.org/10.1111/j.1460-2466.2004.tb02649.x

Braun, S., Hernandez Bark, A., Kirchner, A., Stegmann, S., & Van Dick, R. (2019). Emails from the boss—Curse or blessing? Relations between communication channels, leader evaluation, and employees' attitudes. *International Journal of Business Communication*, *56*(1), 50–81. https://doi.org/10.1177/2329488415597516

Carrière, J., & Bourque, C. (2009). The effects of organizational communication on job satisfaction and organizational commitment in a land ambulance service and the mediating role of communication satisfaction. *Career Development International*, *14*(1), 29–49. https://doi.org/10.1108/13620430910933565

Chia, J. (2005). Measuring the immeasurable? *PRism*, *4*(2), 1–13.

Coyle-Shapiro, J. A. M., Pereira Costa, S., Doden, W., & Chang, C. (2019). Psychological contracts: Past, present, and future. *Annual Review of Organizational Psychology and Organizational Behavior*, *6*, 145–169. https://doi.org/10.1146/annurev-orgpsych-012218-015212

Crescenzo, S. (2011). Integrating employee communications media. In T. Gillis (Ed.), *The IABC handbook of organizational communication: A guide to internal communication, public relations, marketing, and leadership* (pp. 219–230). Wiley.

Cropanzano, R., & Mitchell, M. S. (2005). Social exchange theory: An interdisciplinary review. *Journal of Management, 31*(6), 874–900. https://doi.org/10.1177/0149206305279602

Cropanzano, R., Anthony, E. L., Daniels, S. R., & Hall, A. V. (2017). Social exchange theory: A critical review with theoretical remedies. *The Academy of Management Annals, 11*(1), 479–516. https://doi.org/10.5465/annals.2015.0099

Daft, R. L., & Lengel, R. H. (1984). Information richness: A new approach to managerial behavior and organizational design. *Research in Organizational Behavior, 6*, 191–233.

Daft, R. L., & Lengel, R. H. (1986). Organizational information requirements, media richness and structural design. *Management Science, 32*(5), 554–571.

Dévényi, M. (2016). The role of integrative strategies and tactics in HR negotiations. *Strategic Management, 21*(2), 32–36.

Drenth, P. J. D., Thierry, H., & de Wolff, C. J. (Eds.). (1998). *Organizational psychology*. Psychology Press.

Einwiller, S., Ruppel, C., & Stranzl, J. (2021). Achieving employee support during the COVID-19 pandemic. *Journal of Communication Management, 25*(3), 233–255. https://doi.org/10.1108/jcom-10-2020-0107

Eisenberger, R., Rhoades Shanock, L., & Wen, X. (2020). Perceived organizational support: Why caring about employees counts. *Annual Review of Organizational Psychology and Organizational Behavior, 7*, 101–124. https://doi.org/10.1146/annurev-orgpsych-012119-044917

Friedl, J., & Tkalac Verčič, A. (2011). Media preferences of digital natives' internal communication: A pilot study. *Public Relations Review, 37*(1), 84–86. https://doi.org/10.1016/j.pubrev.2010.12.004

Goldhaber, G. M. (1993). *Organizational communication* (6th ed.). Brown & Benchmark.

Goldhaber, G. M., Yates, M. P., Porter, D. P., & Lesniak, R. (1978). Organizational communication. *Human Communication Research, 5*, 76–96.

Goodman, J., & Truss, C. (2004). The medium and the message: Communicating effectively during a major change initiative. *Journal of Change Management, 4*(3), 217–228. https://doi.org/10.1080/1469701042000255392

Grunig, J. E. (1992). Symmetrical systems of internal communication. In J. Grunig (Ed.), *Excellence in public relations and communication management* (pp. 531–576). Lawrence Erlbaum.

Hargie, O., & Tourish, D. (2009). *Auditing organizational communication*. Routledge.

Helsby, N. (2002). *The rise of the internal communicator: A research report on the role of senior internal communication practitioners conducted in 37 major UK and US businesses*. Watson Helsby. Retrieved from https://www.watsonhelsby.co.uk/assets/files/The-Rise-of-the-Internal-Communicator.pdf

Henderson, J., & McAdam, R. (2003). Adopting a learning-based approach to improve internal communications: A large utility experience. *International Journal of Quality & Reliability Management, 20*(7), 774–794. https://doi.org/10.1108/02656710310491212

Jablin, F. M., & Putnam, L. L. (2001). *The new handbook of organizational communication: Advances theory, research and methods*. Sage Publications.

Jablin, F. M., Putnam, L. L., Roberts, K., & Porter, L. (Eds.). (1987). *Handbook of organizational communication: An interdisciplinary perspective*. SAGE Publications.

Jones, E., Watson, B., Gardner, J., & Gallois, C. (2004). Organizational communication: Challenges for the new century. *Journal of Communication*, *54*(4), 722–750. https://doi.org/10.1111/j.1460-2466.2004.tb02652.x

Kalla, H. K. (2005). Integrated internal communications: A multidisciplinary perspective. *Corporate Communications: An International Journal*, *10*, 302–314. https://doi.org/10.1108/13563280510630106

Kitchen, P. J., & Daly, F. (2002). Internal communication during change management. *Corporate Communications: An International Journal*, *7*(1), 46–53. https://doi.org/10.1108/13563280210416035

Kotter, J. P. (1996). *Leading change*. Harvard Business School Press.

Lee, Y. (2018). Dynamics of symmetrical communication within organizations: The impacts of channel usage of CEO, managers, and peers. *International Journal of Business Communication*, *59*(1), 1–19. https://doi.org/10.1177/2329488418803661

Lee, Y., & Yue, C. A. (2020). Status of internal communication research in public relations: An analysis of published articles in nine scholarly journals from 1970 to 2019. *Public Relations Review*, *46*(3), 1–10. https://doi.org/10.1016/j.pubrev.2020.101906

Lloyd, S. (2002). Branding from the inside out. *BRW*, *24*(10), 64–66.

Lowenberg, G., & Conrad, K. A. (1998). *Current perspectives in industrial/organizational psychology*. Allyn & Bacon.

Mayer, R. C., & Gavin, M. B. (2005). Trust in management and performance: Who minds the shop while the employees watch the boss. *Academy of Management Journal*, *48*(5), 874–888. https://doi.org/10.5465/amj.2005.18803928

McKenzie, T. (2007). Lessons learned about change at sun microsystems. *Strategic Communication Management*, *11*(1), 14–17.

McKinsey Global Institute (2016). *How social media tools can reshape the organization.* Retrieved from https://www.mckinsey.com/business-functions/digital-mckinsey/our-insights/how-social-tools-can-reshape-the-organization

Men, L. R. (2014). Why leadership matters to internal communication: Linking transformational leadership, symmetrical communication, and employee outcomes. *Journal of Public Relations Research*, *26*(3), 256–279. https://doi.org/10.1080/1062726X.2014.908719

Men, L. R., & Yue, C. A. (2019). Creating a positive emotional culture: Effect of internal communication and impact on employee supportive behaviors. *Public Relations Review*, *45*(3), 101764. https://doi.org/10.1016/j.pubrev.2019.03.001

Men, L. R., O'Neil, J., & Ewing, M. (2020). Examining the effects of internal social media usage on employee engagement. *Public Relations Review*, *46*(2), 101880. https://doi.org/10.1016/j.pubrev.2020.101880

Men, R. L., & Bowen, S. A. (2017). *Excellence in internal communication management*. New York, NY: Business Expert Press.

Miller, K. (1996). Who are we and what are we doing? *Management Communication Quarterly*, *10*(1), 3–4. https://doi.org/10.1177/0095399704272403

Mishra, A. K., & Mishra, K. E. (1994). The role of mutual trust in effective downsizing strategies. *Human Resource Management*, *33*(2), 261–279. https://doi.org/10.1002/hrm.3930330207

Mishra, K., & Boynton, L. (2011, January 13). *Talk-the-Talk: Using internal communication to build trust with employees*. Institute for Public Relations. Retrieved from https://instituteforpr.org/wp-content/uploads/Talk-the-Talk.pdf

Mishra, K., Boynton, L., & Mishra, A. (2014). Driving employee engagement: The expanded role of internal communications. *International Journal of Business Communication, 51*(2), 183–202. https://doi.org/10.1177/2329488414525399

Mumby, D. (2007). Organizational communication. In G. Ritzer (Ed.), *The encyclopedia of sociology* (pp. 3290–3299). Blackwell.

Pinnington, A. H. (2003). Organizational culture: Liberation or entrapment? In D. Tourish, & O. Hargie (Eds.), *Key issues in organizational communication* (pp. 205–219). Routledge.

Prasad, A. (2019). Untapped relationship between employer branding, anticipatory psychological contract and intent to join. *Global Business Review, 20*(1), 194–213. https://doi.org/10.1177/0972150917713897

Proctor, T., & Doukakis, I. (2003). Change management: The role of internal communication and employee development. *Corporate Communications, 8*(4), 268–277. https://doi.org/10.1108/13563280310506430

Pugh, S. D., & Dietz, J. (2008). Employee engagement at the organizational level of analysis. *Industrial and Organizational Psychology, 1*(1), 45–48. https://doi.org/10.1111/j.1754-9434.2007.00006.x

Quirke, B. (2008). *Making the connections: Using internal communication to turn strategy into action* (2nd ed.). Gower.

Rhee, Y. (2004). *The employee-public-organization chain in relationship management: A case study of a government organization* [Doctoral dissertation]. ProQuest Dissertations Publishing. https://www.proquest.com/docview/305177510?pq-origsite=gscholar&fromopenview=true

Rhee, Y., & Moon, B. (2009). Organizational culture and strategic communication practice: Testing the competing values model (CVM) and employee communication strategies (ECS) model in Korea. *International Journal of Strategic Communication, 3*(1), 52–67. https://doi.org/10.1080/15531180802608386

Röttger, U., & Voß, A. (2008). Internal communication as management of trust relations: A theoretical framework. In A. Zerfass, B. van Ruler, & K. Sriramesh (Eds.), *Public relations research: European and international perspectives and innovations* (pp. 163–177). VS Verlag für Sozialwissenschaften.

Ruck, K., & Welch, M. (2012). Valuing internal communication; management and employee perspectives. *Public Relations Review, 38*(2), 294–302. https://doi.org/10.1016/j.pubrev.2011.12.016

Sievert, H., & Scholz, C. (2017). Engaging employees in (at least partly) disengaged companies. Results of an interview survey within about 500 German corporations on the growing importance of digital engagement via internal social media. *Public Relations Review, 43*(5), 894–903. https://doi.org/10.1016/j.pubrev.2017.06.001

Šimanskienė, L. (2002). Organizacinės kultūros diagnozavimo problemos. *Organizacijų Vadyba: Sisteminiai Tyrimai, 24*, 171–183.

Sinčić Ćorić, D., & Pološki Vokić, N. (2009). The roles of internal communications, human resource management and marketing concepts in determining holistic internal marketing philosophy. *Zagreb International Review of Economics & Business, 12*(2), 87–105.

Smith, L., & Mounter, P. (2008). *Effective internal communication*. Kogan Page Publishers.

Thompkins, P. K. (1987). Translating organizational theory: Symbolism over substance. In F. M. Jablin, L. L. Putnam, K. H. Roberts, & L. W. Porter (Eds.), *Handbook of organizational communication: An interdisciplinary perspective* (pp. 70–96). Sage.

Tkalac Verčič, A. (2016). *Odnosi s javnošću* [Public Relations]. Print.
Tkalac Verčič, A. (2019). Internal communication with a global perspective. In K. Shriramesh, & D. Verčič (Eds.), *The global public relations handbook theory, research, and practice* (pp. 195–204). Routledge.
Tkalac Verčič, A. (2021). The impact of employee engagement, organisational support and employer branding on internal communication satisfaction. *Public Relations Review*, *47*(1), 102009. https://doi.org/10.1016/j.pubrev.2021.102009
Tkalac Verčič, A., & Pološki Vokić, N. (2017). Engaging employees through internal communication. *Public Relations Review*, *43*(5), 885–893. https://doi.org/10.1016/j.pubrev.2017.04.005
Tkalac Verčič, A., & Špoljarić, A. (2020). Managing internal communication: How the choice of channels affects internal communication satisfaction. *Public Relations Review*, *46*(3), 101926. https://doi.org/10.1016/j.pubrev.2020.101926
Tkalac Verčič, A., & Verčič, D. (2005). Envisioning public relations: Between audits and evaluations. In EUPRERA, *Proceedings of the 7th annual EUPRERA Congress: Public relations, corporate values, social responsibility and social commitment.* EUPRERA.
Tkalac Verčič, A., Galić, Z., & Žnidar, K. (2021). The relationship of internal communication satisfaction with employee engagement and employer attractiveness: Testing the joint mediating effect of the social exchange quality indicators [Advanced online publication]. *International Journal of Business Communication*. https://doi.org/10.1177/23294884211053839
Tkalac Verčič, A., Verčič, D., & Sriramesh, K. (2012). Internal communication: Definition, parameters, and the future. *Public Relations Review*, *38*(2), 223–230. https://doi.org/10.1016/j.pubrev.2011.12.019
Tourish, D. (2007). Review article: Communication, discourse and leadership. *Human Relations*, *60*, 1727–1740. https://doi.org/10.1177/0018726707084306
Tourish, D., & Hargie, O. (2009). *Auditing organizational communication: A handbook of research, theory and practice*. Routledge.
Wehmeier, S., & Winkler, P. (2013). Expanding the bridge, minimizing the gaps: Public relations, organizational communication, and the idea that communication constitutes organization. *Management Communication Quarterly*, *27*(2), 280–290. https://doi.org/10.1177/0893318912469772
Welch, M. (2011). The evolution of the employee engagement concept: Communication implications. *Corporate Communications: An International Journal*, *16*(4), 328–346. https://doi.org/10.1108/13563281111186968
Welch, M. (2012). Appropriateness and acceptability: Employee perspectives of internal communication. *Public Relations Review*, *38*(2), 246–254. https://doi.org/10.1016/j.pubrev.2011.12.017
Welch, M., & Jackson, P. R. (2007). Rethinking internal communication: A stakeholder approach. *Corporate Communications: An International Journal*, *12*(2), 177–198. https://doi.org/10.1108/13563280710744847
Wiley, J. W., Kowske, B. J., & Herman, A. E. (2010). Developing and validating a global model of employee engagement. In S. L. Albrecht (Ed.). *Handbook of employee engagement: Perspectives, issues, research and practice* (pp. 351–363). Edward Elgar. https://doi.org/10.4337/9781849806374.00039
Young, M., & Post, J. E. (1993). Managing to communicate, communicating to manage: How leading companies communicate with employees. *Organizational Dynamics*, *22*(1), 31–43. https://doi.org/10.1016/0090-2616(93)90080-K

Zerfass, A., Tench, R., Verhoeven, P., Verčič, D., & Moreno, A. (2010). *European Communication Monitor 2010: Status quo and challenges for Communication management in Europe. Results of an empirical survey in 46 countries*. EACD & EUPRERA.

Zwijze-Koning, K. H., & de Jong, M. D. T. (2007). Measurement of communication satisfaction: Evaluating the communication satisfaction questionnaire as a communication audit tool. *Management Communication Quarterly*, *20*(3), 261–282. https://doi.org/10.1177/0893318906295680

2 The organizational setting of internal communication

A department's position in the organizational structure defines its importance and influence within the organization. Organizations position internal communication in various ways, depending on the organization's size, its culture, management style, financial resources, employee characteristics, expectations, and structural changes. Many organizations have no separate internal communication function, or even a specialized practitioner. In some organizations, internal communication is part of corporate communication or human resources departments. In some organizations, internal communication is carried out by an independent unit that reports directly to the CEO, corporate communication manager, or human resources manager. In order to contribute as much as possible to organizational success, the practitioners or department responsible for internal communication should be positioned high enough in the organizational structure to influence decision-making (Holtz, 2004; Tkalac Verčič, 2019).

Organizational setting and positioning

Positioning traditionally describes an organization's "position" compared to that of its competitors (Porter, 1980) within the mind of consumers, or any other public for that matter (Trout, 1996). However, like branding, the concept of positioning can be applied to nearly anything (Trout, 1996). (See Chapter 8 for more on branding.) In contrast to branding, which aims to elicit an appropriate perception of an object (organization, its products or services, or an individual), positioning aims to elicit an appropriate perception of an object in comparison to other objects of the same sort (Uggla, 2015).

Just as consumers position organizations and their products in their minds, organizations position their employees and departments within a defined structure (Brockhaus & Zerfass, 2021). This positioning within an organizational structure ultimately defines "systems of communication, systems of authority (or other roles), and systems of workflow" (Leavitt, 1965, p. 1144). Positioning determines a department's or employee's

DOI: 10.4324/9781003200109-2

ability to influence decisions, as well as their power within the organization (Berger & Reber, 2006). Positioning within organizational structure is visually presented as an organizational chart or organigram (Fraser, 1978; Oomes, 2004; Webb, 2018).

Organizational structure, together with other organizational characteristics (Pettigrew, 1979), contributes significantly to organizational success (Zheng et al., 2010) by influencing organizational behavior, which in turn affects an organization's competitive advantage (Robbins & Judge, 2013; Wagner & Hollenbeck, 2020; Ulrich & Lake, 1991). A department's importance is determined by how much it contributes to organizational success and influences an organization's competitive advantage. Proper perception of a department's importance ensures its adequate positioning within the organizational structure (Brockhaus & Zerfass, 2021).

Positioning communication within organizations

Herein lies a major challenge for effective communication, whether internal or external: despite the importance of communication departments within organizations (Gillis, 2006), often they do not have a suitably important position in the structure. The same, in fact, is often true, for other "soft power" departments such as marketing and human resources. These functions often must first "prove their importance" to the organization before they are positioned high enough within the structure to participate in decision-making (Brockhaus & Zerfass, 2021; Falkheimer et al., 2016).

One of the determinants of the position of communication departments within organizations is their legitimacy (Brockhaus & Zerfass, 2021). "Legitimacy is a generalized perception or assumption that the actions of an entity are desirable, proper, or appropriate within some socially constructed system of norms, values, beliefs, and definitions" (Suchman, 1995, p. 574). Just as when individuals adapt their behavior to "meet other people's expectations" in a social environment (Brockhaus & Zerfass, 2021), organizations aim to adopt structures and engage in behaviors that will be perceived by consumers and other publics as desirable, proper, or appropriate in order to be perceived as legitimate (Meyer & Rowan, 1977). The more that communication is perceived to contribute to an organization's legitimacy, the more likely the organization is to assign that function a high place in its structure. In this way, legitimacy is at once a determinant and consequence of the positioning of internal communication in the organizational structure (Brockhaus & Zerfass, 2021; Grandien & Johansson, 2012). Since departments that seek high positioning compete with one another, a communication department's position arises through continuous "negotiation" and "adaptation" as well as relationships within the organization that affect the perception of communication (Brockhaus & Zerfass, 2021).

Positioning internal communication within organizations

Although theory considers internal communication to be a part of public relations (Ruck, 2020), internal communication is not always a part of public relations or corporate communication function. In fact, internal communication units in some organizations report to legal affairs or even finance and accounting (Holtz, 2004). Given that internal communication is "increasingly likely to be associated with employee experience" (Ruck, 2020, p. 21), it is sometimes considered an aspect of human resources management. However, internal communication transcends human resources because one of its key tasks is to position an organization's identity in employees' minds (Holtz, 2004), and therefore it should be given greater importance. Internal communication can be positioned as part of corporate communications, but this function combines internal and external communication and usually prioritizes the latter (Smith & Mounter, 2008). Even so, closely relating internal and external communication can align communication messages and goals (Smith & Mounter, 2008). This reflects that messaging within the organization can mold employee's perceptions and that employees, especially through social media, can act as important gatekeepers and influencers on issues related to their organizations.

Zaumane and Leščevica (2021) reviewed relevant literature and developed a classification for assigning the responsibility for internal communication within an organization, as shown in Figure 2.1.

They noted that internal communication tends to assume a supportive, technical role if it is assigned as part of other responsibilities. If internal communication is to contribute fully to an organization's strategic goals, it requires a certain level of autonomy from, yet coordination with, other departments.

In a survey of nearly 500 European companies with at least 500 employees, Nelli (2018) found that about 60% had stand-alone internal communication departments, while the remaining 40% positioned internal communication within another department, most often corporate communications, followed by the CEO's office, human resources or external communication/public relations (Figure 2.2). Among the responding companies, the internal communication departments in 36% reported to the department of corporate communications, followed by the CEO's office (22%) or to the department of human resources (19%). Among companies with a separate department of internal communications, that unit was staffed by 2–3 people in 41% of companies, 1 person in 28% of companies, 4–6 people in 16% of companies, and larger numbers of people in 15% of companies.

The larger the company was, the more likely it was to have a separate department of internal communication: 83% of companies with more than 5,000 employees had one, compared to 63% of companies with

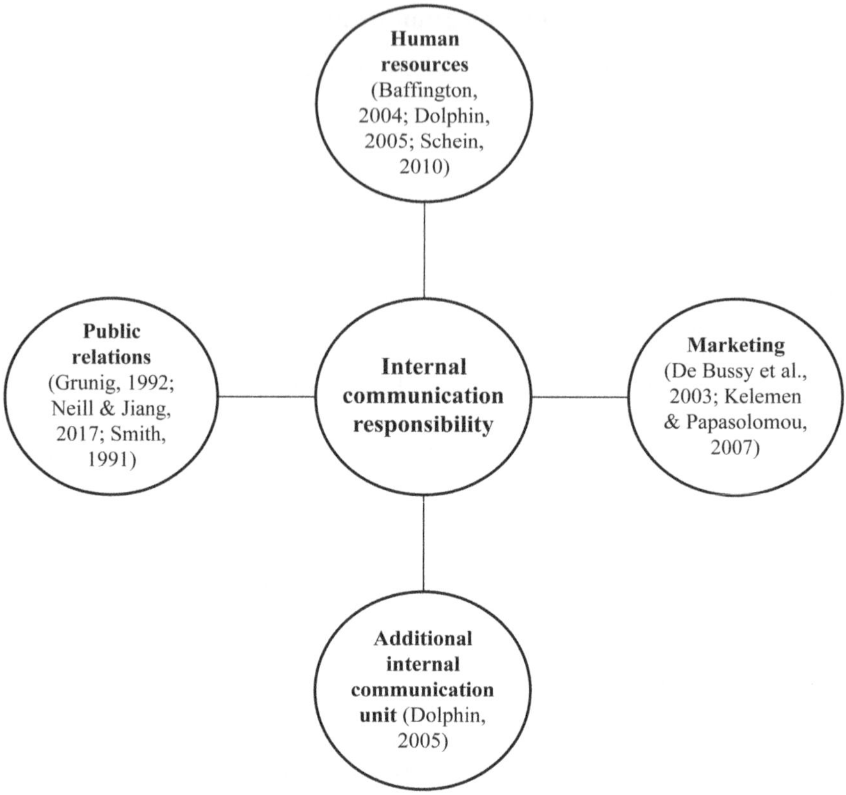

Figure 2.1 Assigning the responsibility for internal communication within an organization.

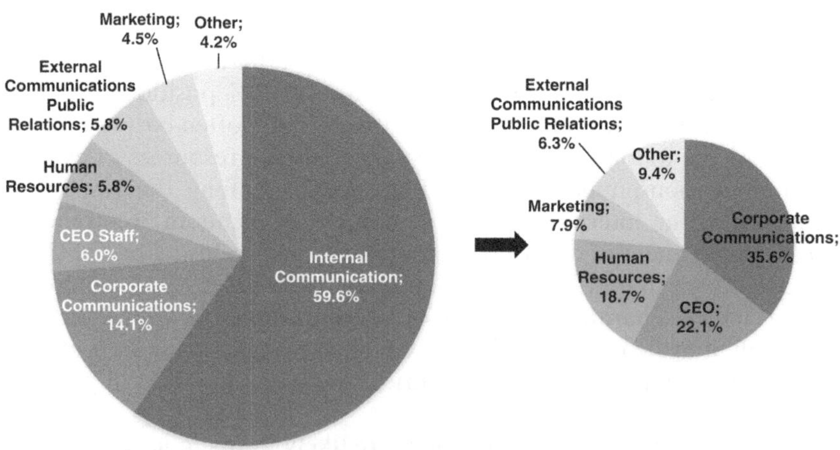

Figure 2.2 Positioning of the internal communication function in 448 European companies with at least 500 employees (Nelli, 2018).

1,001–5,000 employees or 39% of companies with up to 1,000 employees. The more geographically complex a company's operations were, the more likely it was to have a separate department of internal communication: 66% of companies operating at several locations in multiple countries had one, compared to 57% of companies operating at several locations in a single country or 44% of companies operating at one location in a single country.

It is likely that, in the post-COVID-19 world, the importance of internal communication has grown significantly. Indeed, a report from the Chartered Institute of Public Relations (2021) indicates that the quantity of internal communication-related tasks increased by nearly 50% from spring 2020 to spring 2021, based on a survey of public relations practitioners. This leads us to believe that public relations practitioners are taking over internal communication as their own. This may blur the lines between internal and external communication, as Ruck (2020) predicted, even more than social media already have. Practitioners should be wary of this, since internal and external publics have different expectations and needs, and an organization cannot meet them all with a "one-size-fits-all" approach (Macaulay, 2017).

The position of internal communication in our study

One of the goals of the research project from which this book emerged was to explore the activities of internal communication, its positioning within organizations and its contributions to organizational performance, as well as its relationship to employer branding, employee engagement and social exchange quality. Our research included 26 Croatian organizations, some private, others public and still others of mixed public-private ownership. These organizations were selected based on typical unit criteria (Gerring, 2016) determined by the project team, who took into account organizational characteristics such as sector, size, financial and non-financial indicators, and internal communication practices. In the first and second phases of our research, we conducted in-depth interviews with directors of corporate communications and human resources. After the interviews, we asked the participants to provide data on their internal communication channels and to indicate the position of internal communication in their organigrams. We surveyed the general workforce of the participating organizations with questionnaires about socio-demographic characteristics, internal communication satisfaction (Tkalac Verčič et al., 2009, 2021), employer attractiveness (Berthon et al., 2005), employee engagement (Schaufeli et al., 2002), psychological contract fulfillment (Robinson & Morrison, 2000), and organizational support (Eisenberger et al., 1986). Chapter 5 provides further details about our research methods.

We found that among the organizations in our sample, internal communication was not a function on its own, but was part of the daily responsibilities of corporate communications or human resources departments. The organizations differed in how much importance they attached to internal communication activities. None of the five organizations with the lowest internal communication satisfaction ($M < 4.0$) had a designated employee whose primary task was internal communication, and they rarely conducted planned, formal internal communication activities. When they did, such activities were most often organized by someone from corporate communications. In contrast, four of the five organizations with the highest internal communication satisfaction ($M > 5.2$) had at least one person whose job consisted mostly of internal communication, and internal communication was considered to involve collaboration between corporate communications and human resources, with no clear priority of one over the other. In some of these organizations, departments of public relations and corporate communications took the lead in internal communication; in others, human resources took the lead. In all cases, the CEO reported a supportive attitude toward internal communication. This can lead organizations to approach internal communications strategically, which can increase their effectiveness (Smith & Mounter, 2008).

Among the 26 organizations in our study, two emerged as outliers because they had a separate internal communications unit. In both, the level of internal communication satisfaction exceeded the average of 4.7 across all 26 organizations. In one of these outliers, Organization A, internal communication was a part of corporate communications, but this department contained one employee with the title of "internal communication director", whose sole responsibility was internal communication (Figure 2.3). The director managed a team of six whose primary

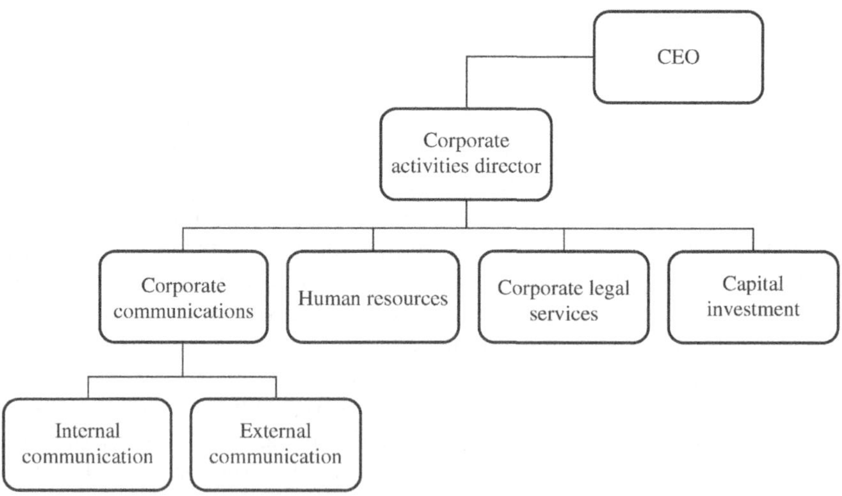

Figure 2.3 The position of internal communication within Organization A in our study.

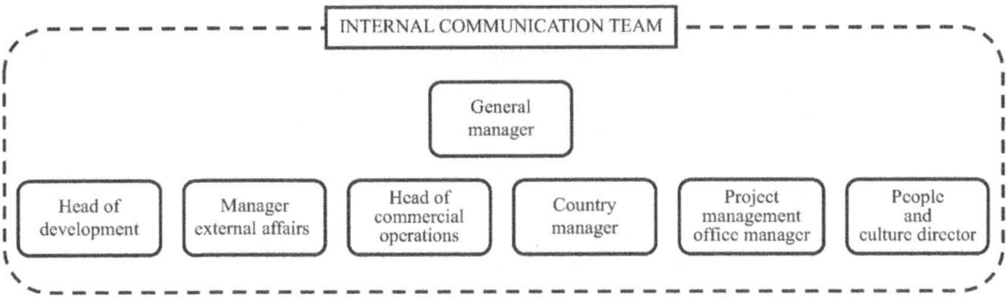

Figure 2.4 Internal communication team in Organization B in our study.

responsibility was internal communication, but who also conducted other corporate communication tasks when necessary.

In the other outlier, Organization B, internal communication was conducted by a team of six people, supervised by a general manager. Each team member directed his or her own organizational unit but also planned and coordinated internal communication activities within the entire organization (Figure 2.4). Our interviewees from this organization explained that internal communication was positioned in the organigram in this way in order to ensure that it encompassed all relevant information and activities. Those interviewees emphasized the need for segmenting the internal publics, something we did not encounter in the other organizations in our study.

Conclusion – preferred positioning of internal communication

Holtz (2004), Smith and Mounter (2008), and Tkalac Verčič (2019) concur in that internal communication should be positioned at the top of an organization, with the internal communication director reporting directly to the CEO. Based on the research project from which this book emerged, we recommend that the internal communication director have a background in public relations or strategic communication. While informal internal communication should be encouraged, formal internal communication should be managed strategically. Thus, the internal communication team should have backgrounds in public relations and human resources.

References

Berger, B. K., & Reber, B. H. (2006). *Gaining influence in public relations: The role of resistance in practice*. Routledge.

Berthon, P., Ewing, M., & Hah, L. L. (2005). Captivating company: Dimensions of attractiveness in employer branding. *International Journal of Advertising*, *24*(2), 151–172. https://doi.org/10.1080/02650487.2005.11072912

Brockhaus, J., & Zerfass, A. (2021). Strengthening the role of communication departments: A framework for positioning communication departments at the top of and throughout organizations. *Corporate Communications: An International Journal*, *27*(1), 53–70. https://doi.org/10.1108/CCIJ-02-2021-0021

Buffington, J. (2004). Can human resources and internal communication peacefully coexist? *Internal Communication*, *10*(4), 33–35.

Chartered Institute of Public Relations. (2021). *PR in a Pandemic: A CIPR report exploring the impact of the COVID-19 pandemic on the public relations profession*. Retrieved from https://cipr.co.uk/CIPR/Our_work/Policy/CIPR_State_of_the_Profession_2019_20.asp

De Bussy, N. M., Ewing, M. T., & Pitt, L. F. (2003). Stakeholder theory and internal marketing communications: A framework for analysing the influence of new media. *Journal of Marketing Communications*, *9*(3), 147–161. https://doi.org/10.1080/1352726032000129890

Dolphin, R. R. (2005). Internal communication: today's strategic imperative. *Journal of Marketing Communications*, *11*(3), 171–190.

Eisenberger, R., Huntington, R., Hutchison, S., & Sowa, D. (1986). Perceived organizational support. *Journal of Applied Psychology*, *71*(3), 500–507. https://doi.org/10.1037/0021-9010.71.3.500

Falkheimer, J., Heide, M., Simonsson, C., Zerfass, A., & Verhoeven, P. (2016). Doing the right things or doing things right? Paradoxes and Swedish communication professionals' roles and challenges. *Corporate Communications: An International Journal*, *21*(2), 142–159. https://doi.org/10.1108/CCIJ-06-2015-0037

Fraser, R. (1978). Reorganizing the organization chart. *Public Administration Review*, *38*(3), 280–282. https://doi.org/975683

Gerring, J. (2016). *Case study research: Principles and practices*. Cambridge University Press.

Gillis, T. L. (Ed.). (2006). *The IABC handbook of organizational communication: A guide to internal communication, public relations, marketing, and leadership*. Jossey-Bass.

Grandien, C., & Johansson, C. (2012). Institutionalization of communication management: A theoretical framework. *Corporate Communications: An International Journal*, *17*(2), 209–227. https://doi.org/10.1108/13563281211220247

Grunig, J. E. (Ed.) (1992). *Excellence in public relations and communication management*. Hillsdale: Lawrence Erlbaum Associates, Publisher.

Holtz, S. (2004). *Corporate conversations: A guide to crafting effective and appropriate internal communication*. American Management Association.

Kelemen, M., & Papasolomou, I. (2007). Internal marketing: A qualitative study of culture change in the UK banking sector. *Journal of Marketing Management*, *23*(7–8), 746–768. https://doi.org/10.1362/026725707X230027

Leavitt, H. J. (1965). Applied organizational change in industry: Structural, technological, and humanistic approaches. In J. March (Ed.), *Handbook of organizations* (pp. 1144–1170). Rand McNally & Company.

Macaulay, K. (2017). *How to Tackle the Blurring Lines Between Internal and External Communication*. International Association of Business Communicators Boston. Retrieved from http://boston.iabc.com/2017/11/13/how-to-tackle-the-blurring-lines-between-internal-and-external-communication/

Meyer, J. W., & Rowan, B. (1977). Institutionalized organizations: Formal structure as myth and ceremony. *American Journal of Sociology*, *83*(2), 340–363. https://doi.org/10.1086/226550

Neill, M. S., & Jiang, H. (2017). Functional silos, integration & encroachment in internal communication. *Public Relations Review*, *43*(4), 850–862. https://doi.org/10.1016/j.pubrev.2017.06.009

Nelli, R. P. (2018). *Internal communication in Europe: Key success factors and managerial approaches*. Vita e Pansiero.

Oomes, A. H. J. (2004). Organization awareness in crisis management: Dynamic organigrams for more effective disaster response. In B. Carle, & B. Van de Walle (Eds.), *Proceedings of ISCRAM2004* (pp. 63–68). ISCRAM. http://idl.iscram.org/files/oomes/2004/178_Oomes2004.pdf

Pettigrew, A. M. (1979). On studying organizational cultures. *Administrative Science Quarterly*, *24*(4), 570–581. https://doi.org/2392363

Porter, M. E. (1980). Industry structure and competitive strategy: Keys to profitability. *Financial Analysts Journal*, *36*(4), 30–41. https://doi.org/10.2469/faj.v36.n4.30

Robbins, S. P., & Judge, T. A. (2013). *Organizational behavior* (18th ed.). Pearson Education.

Robinson, S. L., & Morrison, E. W. (2000). The development of psychological contract breach and violation: A longitudinal study. *Journal of Organizational Behavior*, *21*(5), 525–546. https://doi.org/10.1002/1099-1379(200008)21:5<525::AID-JOB40>3.0.CO;2-T

Ruck, K. (2020). Theoretical and practical positioning of internal communication. In K. Ruck (Ed.), *Exploring internal communication: Towards informed employee voice* (pp. 15–24). Routledge.

Schaufeli, W. B., Salanova, M., González-Romá, V., & Bakker, A. B. (2002). The measurement of engagement and burnout: A two sample confirmatory factor analytic approach. *Journal of Happiness Studies*, *3*(1), 71–92. https://doi.org/10.1023/A:1015630930326

Schein, E. H. (2010). The role of organization development in the human resources function. *OD Practitioner*, *42*(4), 6–11.

Smith, A. (1991). *Innovative employee communication: New approaches to improving trust, teamwork and performance*. Prentice Hall.

Smith, L., & Mounter, P. (2008). *Effective internal communication* (2nd ed.). Kogan Page Publishers.

Suchman, M. C. (1995). Managing legitimacy: Strategic and institutional approaches. *Academy of Management Review*, *20*(3), 571–610. https://doi.org/10.5465/amr.1995.9508080331

Tkalac Verčič, A. (2019). Internal communication with a global perspective. In K. Sriramesh & D. Verčič (Eds.), *The global public relations handbook: Theory, research, and practice* (3rd ed., pp. 195–204). Routledge.

Tkalac Verčič, A., Pološki Vokić, N., & Sinčić Ćorić, D. (2009). Razvoj mjernog instrumenta za procjenu zadovoljstva internom komunikacijom [Development of the internal communication satisfaction questionnaire]. *Društvena istraživanja: časopis za opća društvena pitanja*, *18*(1–2), 175–202.

Tkalac Verčič, A., Sinčić Ćorić, D., & Pološki Vokić, N. (2021). Measuring internal communication satisfaction: Validating the internal communication satisfaction questionnaire. *Corporate Communications: An International Journal*, *26*(3), 589–604. https://doi.org/10.1108/CCIJ-01-2021-0006

Trout, J. (1996). *The new positioning: The latest on the World's #1 business strategy*. McGraw-Hill.

Uggla, H. (2015). Positioning in the mind versus brand extension: The revision of Ries and Trout. *IUP Journal of Brand Management*, *12*(1), 35–44.

Ulrich, D., & Lake, D. (1991). Organizational capability: Creating competitive advantage. *Academy of Management Perspectives*, *5*(1), 77–92. https://doi.org/10.5465/ame.1991.4274728

Wagner, J. A., & Hollenbeck, J. R. (2020). *Organizational behavior: Securing competitive advantage*. Routledge.

Webb, J. (2018). Designing Participation with Talk Around an Organigram. In J. Schaeffer, Chirumalla, & B. Clark (Eds.), *Participatory innovation conference 2018 conference proceedings* (pp. 219–226). PIN-C. Retrieved from http://pin-c.sdu.dk/2018.html

Zaumane, I., & Leščevica (2021). Functional responsibility for internal communication management and its integration in contemporary business [Advanced online publication]. *International Journal of Organizational Analysis*. https://doi.org/10.1108/IJOA-06-2021-2822

Zheng, W., Yang, B., & McLean, G. N. (2010). Linking organizational culture, structure, strategy, and organizational effectiveness: Mediating role of knowledge management. *Journal of Business Research*, *63*(7), 763–771. https://doi.org/10.1016/j.jbusres.2009.06.005

3 Strategizing internal communication

Internal communication is simultaneously one of the aspects of management and an emerging organizational function in its own right. The extent to which it occupies its own separate place within an organization depends on the organization's size, maturity, industrial sector, and other factors. Few organizations have separate internal communication departments, and many lack any specialists in internal communication. In most organizations, internal communication is unlikely to be guided by formal strategy or optimized to advance strategic goals. Nevertheless, all organizations use internal communication to influence the knowledge, emotions, and behaviors of their employees.

Management and internal communication

Communication is a central concept in management (Thompkins, 1987). As van Ruler and Verčič (2005) note: "Managers are the ones who are responsible for the communication policies of an organization and the way in which (members of) an organization communicate" (p. 241). Early theorizing about management focused in large part on channels of communication, whether hierarchical or lateral, formal or informal, oral or written for the purposes of persuading, inculturating, influencing decision-making or soliciting feedback (Barnard, 1938/1968; Fayol, 1925/1949; Likert, 1961; Taylor, 1911/1947; Weber, 1947). Mintzberg (1973) found that managers spent two-thirds of their time communicating.

Management and communication are complex processes and difficult to define. Cole (1996) suggested that management could be approached from four "clusters" of perspectives: classical theories, schools of human relations and social psychology, systems and contingency approaches, and modern approaches. Each cluster prioritizes certain communication concepts (van Ruler & Verčič, 2005): classic management theories favor informational approaches to communication; human relations-based theories, persuasive approaches; systems-based theories, relational approaches; and modern theories, the dialogue model. Each of these management-communication dyads tries to solve its own problem: classical

DOI: 10.4324/9781003200109-3

theories examine informational knowledge, human relations-based theories explore persuasive influence, systems-based theories focus on relational trust, and modern theories analyze dialogic meanings.

Classical theories of management (Fayol, 1925/1949; Taylor, 1911/1947) focused on the division and analysis of work, as well as the selection and training of the best available workers to achieve results efficiently. In information theory, which conceptualized organizations as machines (Lasswell, 1948; Shannon & Weaver, 1949), communication was transmission of messages from a sender (management) to a receiver (employees) through a channel that might be distorted by noise and that could be controlled via feedback. Communication, which was primarily unidirectional (top-down), sought to inform and educate through "objective" messages. As a result, the "subjective" implications of messages, such as the emotional reactions that they might elicit in workers, were not a concern for theorists but, instead, distorting influences to be avoided. In all communication, management was perceived as active and employees as passive. In this regard, human resources were conceptualized similarly as financial or material resources.

Human relations and social psychological schools of management (Likert, 1961; Maslow, 1943) stipulated that organizations are more like organisms than machines, and that employees are active in communication. In addition, those schools argued that messages are interpreted not by individuals but by teams or workgroups. They held that optimizing organizational performance did not mean simply selecting and training employees, but also motivating them in line with their own needs and aspirations. This line of thinking led to the persuasive school of communication (Miller, 1989), which focused less on beliefs and cognitions, and more on "attitudes in and around organizations" (Brief, 1998).

Systems and contingency approaches to management (Katz & Kahn, 1966; Lawrence & Lorsch, 1967) merged the "hard" (mechanical) elements of organizations with "soft" (organic) elements, conceptualizing organizational performance as the result of "objective" factors (technical and economic) as well as "subjective" factors, namely humans. In this approach, the challenge of management is to create the right fit among the various elements in organizations, and between organizations and their external environments. This vision of organizations draws on the relational approach to communication (Ledingham & Bruning, 2000). Management must use communication constantly to negotiate with employees and create meaning in order to secure and maintain their active participation. Management and employees are complementary, and the purpose of internal communication is to avoid conflict and ensure collaboration (Ehling, 1992).

Modern approaches to management go beyond issues of efficiency ("doing things right") and ask questions about effectiveness ("doing the right things"). These approaches concern themselves more with values and culture, management of change and transformation, implementation of total quality management and achievement of excellence (Mintzberg, 1989; Peters & Waterman, 1982). Dissensus is valued as much as consensus, because communication is used for "creation of as many meanings as possible" (van Ruler & Verčič, 2005, p. 250), enabling organizations to respond to variability in their environments and visualize different possible futures (see Heath, 2001, 2006).

As these various management approaches illustrate, internal communication can perform different functions in different managerial frameworks, from information and persuasion to negotiation and creation of meaning. In this way, internal communication is an integral part of management: even if managers lack a formal strategy for such communication, they strive to communicate strategically. Perhaps precisely because internal communication is such a fundamental part of management, its status as a separate organizational function has long been neglected. This book and the larger research project from which it arises are an attempt to flesh out the dimensions and potential of internal communication for empowering organizations. As Men (2021) wrote: "In essence, internal communication is both a management function and public relations specialization. It is strategic in nature which aims to achieve specific internal communication goals that contribute to organizational effectiveness. Hence, internal communication can be more appropriately coined as 'strategic internal communication', which is distinct from a similar but easily confused term, organizational communication" (pp. 3–4).

Differentiation of internal communication

The earliest internal communication specialists were journalists and editors of internal communication organs, which were originally limited to internal newspapers and magazines, but later expanded to include radio, television, and multimedia systems. The first professional organizations of "industrial journalists" appeared in the 1930s, such as the American Association of Industrial Editors in 1938, which in 1970 rebranded themselves as business communicators and internal communication specialists (www.iabc.com). In Europe, industrial journalists and editors organized in the late 1940s into a group that would later become the European Association for Internal Communication (www.feiea.eu). Although these developments in the USA and Europe signaled the technical differentiation of internal communication from other corporate and organizational activities, other parts of the organization – general managers, corporate communications, human relations, marketing – still decided what communication channels should be used and what content should be disseminated.

As organizations have grown in size and become more complex and more multi-national and multi-cultural (Tkalac Verčič et al., 2012), what started as a purely journalistic function of technically managing communication from management toward employees, has evolved into strategic, multi-channel management in all directions, whether top-down, down-up, horizontal, diagonal, circular or fuzzy. Effective managers of all these communication processes are essential: large organizations may employ dozens of internal communication specialists and have substantial budgets, and the increasingly abstract and complex goals of such communication must be managed as carefully and strategically as other intangible capital.

Most large organizations in the 21st century recognize the need for a specialist internal communication function, to which they are beginning to assign strategic importance. Researchers are launching investigations into what makes internal communication specific and different from other communication functions, such as corporate and marketing communications or public affairs (Helsby, 2002; Tkalac Verčič et al., 2012; Zaumane & Leščevica, 2021). This book, and the larger research project from which it arises, is an example of that. Universities and business schools are developing academic courses in internal communication, preparing future practitioners to assume important positions in organizations. All this speaks to the development of internal communication into a separate discipline.

Despite the central role of internal communication in an organization's success, management may choose, as our interviewee noted, to concern itself "with other things". However, organizations with better internal communication outperform otherwise similar organizations, showing higher productivity, lower absenteeism and fewer strikes, higher quality of services and products, greater innovation, and lower total operating expenses (Clampitt & Downs, 1993). Good internal communication is, therefore, good for business.

The organizational leadership should therefore recognize that internal communication is essential for effective operation and growth. This essential function should be subject to the same analysis, planning, implementation and evaluation that are applied to all other sensitive functions. In start-ups and micro-organizations, internal communication may arise entirely from the founders or owners and spread osmotically through the small structure. However, as an organization grows, leaders can no longer communicate continuously with everyone else, so internal communication should become the responsibility of a dedicated professional. Such a person may initially handle both internal and external communication, but as the organization grows, the two types of communication should be differentiated, given that they involve "different strategies and tactics which all have a main goal of improving communication within an organization" (Tkalac Verčič, 2021, p. 247).

The European Communication Monitor, the world's largest survey of public relations and communication management, reported in 2009 that 74% of the more than 1,850 respondents from 34 countries indicated that "training managers to act as communicators" was the most urgent need for the field of internal communication (Zerfass et al., 2009, p. 80). The need for such training is even more important given that the professional European communicators who responded to the survey consider that employees have become the most important digital gatekeepers in European organizations (Zerfass et al., 2013), and that "[b]uilding and maintaining trust" in organizations and their leaders is the most important strategic issue for communication management and public relations (Zerfass et al., 2020).

Once internal communication is differentiated from external communication to stand on its own, organizations should ensure that the separate function commands sufficient influence at the decision-making table. Unless top management understands and accepts the importance of internal communication, organizations may fail to muster the people and resources needed for the communication to make a real difference. In his survey of 448 European companies with at least 500 employees, Nelli (2018) found that 60% of companies had a separate internal communication position in the organigram, but only 16% had a formal internal communication plan and monitored how much that function achieved its objectives. Instead, internal communication in most organizations played a merely supportive role, with the department of corporate communications or other units defining objectives. Tkalac Verčič (2019) found a similar situation: "Most internal communication practitioners are not awarded management status and report to corporate communications or (slightly less often) to human resource management" (p. 198).

Strategizing about internal communication should proceed "bottom-up", beginning from the desired impacts for the organization. Managers should be required to demonstrate at least a minimal skill in internal communication, and organizations as a whole should aim to exercise a minimum of such skill as part of their mission to achieve excellence without destroying their human capital.

Strategic internal communication

Strategy originated in warfare: in ancient Greek, it meant the art of the general for winning military conflicts. It stipulates the best ways to achieve the goals and objectives, and it is contingent: the best ways depend on the context (Ruler & Körver, 2019; Rumelt, 2011). Managers can develop a strategy of internal communication to guide their efforts to educate and engage employees, build trust in them toward the organization, and help them find meaning in their work and in their place within the organization. Such a strategy can help managers optimize the distribution of limited resources to achieve the desired outcomes. Internal communication is by itself strategic, because it is "purposeful" and aims to help "an organization fulfill its mission" (Hallahan et al., 2007, p. 3).

Developing an effective strategy can involve taking account of strengths, weaknesses, opportunities, and threats (SWOT). Regardless of how strategies are developed, they can deviate more or less from reality: Mintzberg and Waters (1985) speak of *intended* strategies, which are what managers initially plan; *deliberate* strategies, which are plans that become reality; *emergent* strategies, which may have not been planned, but can be realized based on patterns of previous behavior; and *realized* strategies, which are the sum of deliberate and emergent strategies. When strategizing, a manager's intentions do not necessarily become reality.

Developing strategies for effective internal communication starts from considering the organization in which the communication occurs. Morgan (1986) suggests that organizations can be perceived through eight metaphors: machines, organisms, brains, cultures, political systems, psychiatric prisons, flux and transformation, or instruments of domination. Each metaphor implies a different concept and strategy for internal communication. The strategizing itself can follow several different routes. Mintzberg et al. (1989), for example, deconstructed the notion of strategic management into 10 schools, each of which views strategy formation as a different type of process: conception in the case of the design school, a formal process in the planning school, an analytical process in the positioning school, a visionary process in the entrepreneurial school, a mental process in the cognitive school, an emergent process in the learning school, a process of negotiation in the power school, a collective process in the cultural school, a reactive process in the environmental school, or a process of transformation in the configuration school. All these metaphors and schools must be taken into account to conceptualize internal communication and strategize about it.

Gulbrandsen and Just (2020) approach strategic communication as a performative process in which "communication strategies as well as strategic communication come into being in and through the process of strategizing; they are the result rather than the cause of performances" (p. 33). Internal communication strategies therefore rarely emerge from a distinct managerial planning process; instead, they arise through continuous, sometimes informal strategizing. As one of the interviewees in our research project noted: "I think that we are one of the rare companies in which internal communication doesn't flow from management toward employees; frequently our [communication] department has a role to deliver to the management what is happening in the organization. Management is often separated from the real life in the company because it is dealing with something else". This situation is unlikely to be unusual.

As a result, even though what people informally discuss during a coffee break or over lunch can rarely be relevant for official internal communication, explications of organizational vision and mission as well as the strategies to enact them are important to all members of the organizations.

Communication within an organization is strategic when it is important, significant and "substantial for the survival and sustained success of an entity", in which case we can speak of strategic internal communication. Strategic internal communication is "the purposeful use of communication by [and in] an organization or other entity to engage in conversations of strategic significance to its goals" (Zerfass et al., 2018, p. 493). Members of organizations are not "internal masses", but structured "publics" who are interested in discussing what is happening with the organization. These publics form their cultures and counter-cultures, so communicative life in organizations is always alive and has the potential to support or oppose the organizational mission.

These ideas have several implications. In contrast to organizational communication, internal communication inevitably involves strategy. Organizations conduct internal communication to produce desired results and to achieve desired organizational outcomes. The outcomes may be information and education, persuasion and motivation, dialogue, negotiation and trust, and creation of meaning. But for internal communication to have some value for the organization, it must have an impact on the life of the organization. This is what it means to say that internal communication is purposeful communication.

Many events of internal communication happen at an operational level, such as dissemination of information or solicitation of feedback. Many daily communications related to work, sometimes collectively referred to as managerial communication, are important for everyday life in the organization, although not immediately essential to the organization's survival and growth. Even so, the "sum" of all these small events can take on strategic importance over time. Similarly, an in-house magazine is usually more of tactical than strategic importance, yet during major events such as crises, mergers or acquisitions, it can also become a strategic tool. Definitely strategic are the questions of which communication channels an organization will use, for what purposes and with what budget.

Strategic internal communication is interactive, two-way or – even better – multi-way. Through such communication, an organization discusses what it is doing, what it *should* be doing, and how it can close the gap between them. This communication can take place more or less hierarchically, depending on the organizational culture, characteristics of the top leaders, and characteristics of the industry sector.

With the growing digitalization of communication, strategic internal communication must take care to protect not only organizational interests but also the legal rights of workers to privacy. Many workers use the same smartphone, tablet or laptop for work and leisure, which makes it challenging for organizations to comply with data protection legislation, such as the General Data Protection Regulation in the European Union (https://ec.europa.eu/info/law/law-topic/data-protection_en). There may be additional relevant regulations, such as the rule in France and Portugal that employers cannot send messages to their employees outside work hours. In addition, this situation, coupled with the increasing emphasis on "home office" since the start of the COVID-19 pandemic, exposes workers to communication overload and to a blurring of the line between work and leisure. In short, profound changes in how organizations communicate with their employees, and how employees communicate with one another, are bringing new risks and possibilities for internal communication, which would be best managed by professionally trained internal communicators.

Conclusion

Internal communication has traditionally been viewed as something that happens while people work. With the emergence of management in large organizations, the importance of internal communication began to be recognized, but it was only in the late 20th century that scholars and practitioners of management and communication began to recognize it as a separate function and discipline. It is difficult to imagine an excellent organization in which internal communication is poor: organizations with better internal communication perform better than otherwise similar organizations. Thus, good internal communication can be taken as a sign of good management.

Because of its importance for organizational outcomes, internal communication is strategic by its very nature. Even if its strategies are not formally planned or written down, internal communication must be understood as a central function of strategic management. It can be developed consciously, or it can emerge naturally through social interaction and work processes within the organization. Formalizing the planning of internal communication has several benefits: the relevant strategies and goals can be discussed, monitored and controlled more easily by management in collaboration with employees; and the effectiveness of such communication can more easily be measured and evaluated. Such strategic management of internal communication can lead to reflection and learning that can advance an organization's success and growth.

References

Barnard, C. I. (1938/1968). *The functions of the executive*. Harvard University Press.

Brief, A. P. (1998). *Attitudes in and around organizations*. Sage.

Clampitt, P. G., & Downs, C. W. (1993). Employee perceptions of the relationship between communication and productivity: A field study. *The Journal of Business Communication, 30*(1), 5–29. https://doi.org/10.1177/002194369303000101

Cole, G. A. (1996). *Management: Theory and practice* (5th ed.). Continuum.
Ehling, W. P. (1992). Estimating the value of public relations and communication to an organization. In J. E. Grunig (Ed.), *Excellence in public relations and communication management* (pp. 617–638). Lawrence Erlbaum Associates.
Fayol, H. (1925/1949). *General and industrial management*. Pitman.
Gulbrandsen, I. T., & Just, S. N. (2020). *Strategizing communication: Theory and practice* (2nd ed.). Samfundslitteratur.
Hallahan, K., Holtzhausen, D., van Ruler, B., Verčič, D., & Sriramesh, K. (2007). Defining strategic communication. *International Journal of Strategic Communication, 1*(1), 3–35. https://doi.org/10.1080/15531180701285244
Heath, R. L. (2001). A rhetorical enactment rationale for public relations: The good organization communicating well. In R. L. Heath (Ed.), *Handbook of public relations* (pp. 31–50). Sage.
Heath, R. L. (2006). A rhetorical theory approach to issues management. In C. H. Botan, & V. Hazleton (Eds.), *Public relations theory II* (pp. 63–99). Lawrence Erlbaum Associates.
Helsby, N. (2002). *The rise of the internal communicator: A research report on the role of senior internal communication practitioners conducted in 37 major UK and US businesses*. Watson Helsby. Retrieved from https://www.watsonhelsby.co.uk/assets/files/The-Rise-of-the-Internal-Communicator.pdf
Katz, D., & Kahn, R. L. (1966). *The social psychology of organizations*. Wiley.
Lasswell, H. D. (1948). The structure and function of communication in society. In L. Bryson (Ed.), *The communication of ideas* (pp. 37–52). The Institute for Religious and Social Studies.
Lawrence, P. R., & Lorsch, J. W. (1967). *Organizations and environment*. Harvard University Press.
Ledingham, J. A., & Bruning, S. D. (Eds.). (2000). *Public relations as relationship management: A relational approach to the study and practice of public relations*. Lawrence Erlbaum associates.
Likert, R. (1961). *New patterns of management*. McGraw-Hill.
Maslow, A. H. (1943). A theory of human motivation. *Psychological Review, 50*(4), 370–396. https://doi.org/10.1037/h0054346
Men, L. R. (2021). Evolving research and practice in internal communication. In L. J. Men, & A. T. Verčič (Eds.), *Current trends and issues in internal communication: Theory and practice* (pp. 1–18). Palgrave Macmillan.
Miller, G. R. (1989). Persuasion and public relations: Two "Ps" in a pod. In C. H. Botan, & V. Hazleton (Eds.), *Public relations theory* (pp. 45–66). Lawrence Erlbaum Associates.
Mintzberg, H. (1973). *The nature of managerial work*. Harper & Row.
Mintzberg, H. (1989). *Mintzberg on management: Inside our strange world of organizations*. The Free Press.
Mintzberg, H., & Waters, J. A. (1985). Of strategies, deliberate and emergent. *Strategic Management Journal, 6*(3), 257–272. https://doi.org/10.1002/smj.4250060306
Mintzberg, H., Ahlstrand, B., & Lampel, J. (1989). *Strategy safari: A guided tour through the wilds of strategic management*. The Free Press.
Morgan, G. (1986). *Images of organizations*. Sage.
Nelli, R. P. (2018). *Internal communication in Europe: Key success factors and managerial approaches*. Vita e Pensiero.
Peters, T. J., & Waterman, R. T. Jr. (1982). *In search of excellence: Lessons from America's best-run companies*. Harper & Row.

Ruler, B., & Körver, F. (2019). *The communication strategy handbook: Toolkit for creating a winning strategy*. Peter Lang.

van Ruler, B., & Verčič, D. (2005). Reflective communication management, future ways for public relations research. In P. J. Kalbfleisch (Ed.), *Communication yearbook 29* (pp. 239–273). Lawrence Erlbaum Associates.

Rumelt, R. P. (2011). *Good strategy, bad strategy: The difference and why it matters*. Crown Business.

Shannon, C. E., & Weaver, W. (1949). *A mathematical model of communication*. University of Illinois Press.

Taylor, F. F. W. (1911/1947). *Principles of scientific management*. Harper.

Thompkins, P. K. (1987). Translating organizational theory: Symbolism over substance. In F. M. Jablin, L. L. Putnam, K. H. Roberts, & L. W. Porter (Eds.), *Handbook of organizational communication: An interdisciplinary perspective* (pp. 70–96). Sage.

Tkalac Verčič, A. (2019). Internal communication with a global perspective. In K. Sriramesh & D. Verčič (Eds.), *The global public relations handbook: Theory, research, and practice* (3rd ed., pp. 195–204). Routledge.

Tkalac Verčič, A. (2021). Closing thoughts and future directions. In L. J. Men, & A. Tkalac Verčič (Eds.), *Current trends and issues in internal communication: Theory and practice* (pp. 241–258). Palgrave Macmillan.

Tkalac Verčič, A., Verčič, D., & Sriramesh, K. (2012). Internal communication: Definition, parameters, and the future. *Public Relations Review*, *38*(2), 223–230. https://doi.org/10.1016/j.pubrev.2011.12.019

Weber, M. (1947). *The theory of social and economic organization*. The Free Press.

Zaumane, I., & Leščevica (2021). Functional responsibility for internal communication management and its integration in contemporary business [Advanced online publication]. *International Journal of Organizational Analysis*. https://doi.org/10.1108/IJOA-06-2021-2822

Zerfass, A., Moreno, A., Tench, R., Verčič, D., & Verhoeven, P. (2009). *European Communication Monitor 2009: Trends in communication management and public relations – Results of a survey in 34 countries (Chart version)*. EUPRERA. Retrieved from www.communicationmonitor.eu

Zerfass, A., Moreno, A., Tench, R., Verčič, D., & Verhoeven, P. (2013). *European Communication Monitor 2013. A changing landscape – Managing crises, digital communication and CEO positioning in Europe. Results of a survey in 43 countries*. EACD & EUPRERA.

Zerfass, A., Verčič, D., Nothhaft, H., & Page Werder, K. (2018). Strategic communication: Defining the field and its contribution to research and practice. *International Journal of Strategic Communication*, *12*(4), 487–505. https://doi.org/10.1080/1553118X.2018.1493485

Zerfass, A., Verhoeven, P., Moreno, A., Tench, R., & Verčič, D. (2020). *European Communication Monitor 2020. Ethical challenges, gender issues, cyber security, and competence gaps in strategic communication. Results of a survey in 44 countries*. EACD & EUPRERA.

4 Channels of internal communication

Recent technological advances have triggered particularly disruptive upheavals in society, including in the way people communicate with one another, and by extension in the way modern organizations reach their publics (Tkalac Verčič & Špoljarić, 2020). Today, internal publics of an organization can be reached through traditional face-to-face communication, printed publications, and diverse digital communication channels. These possibilities create a new challenge for organizations: internal communication practitioners need to determine the right set of communication channels to reach different internal segments. When choosing communication channels, organizations should consider their own goals and resources, the needs and preferences of the intended receiver, data transfer speed, and the characteristics of the message itself. In the research project giving rise to this book, we examined the different channels that organizations use and the ways in which they use them. In this chapter, we provide an overview of possible internal communication channels and illustrate the importance of choosing the right mix of channels.

Channels for internal communication

Communication channels are the means for transmitting a message (Tkalac Verčič, 2016). Based on Harrison's (1995) adaptation of Shannon and Weaver's (1949) communication process model, communication processes within organizations consist of nine elements (Figure 4.1) (Fawkes, 2012). The participants in these processes are the *sender* and *receiver*, while the means are the *message* and the *channel*. Within these processes there are four subprocesses: coding, decoding, response, and feedback. Noise is any type of interference that prevents the message from being received or properly understood.

Often, more than one channel is used to deliver the same message, with the intent of reaching different internal segments, equivalent to when marketing campaigns employ a mix of channels and messages to reach multiple audiences. Not exploiting a combination of channels increases the risk that a message will not reach its intended receiver (Wright & Robertson, 2009).

DOI: 10.4324/9781003200109-4

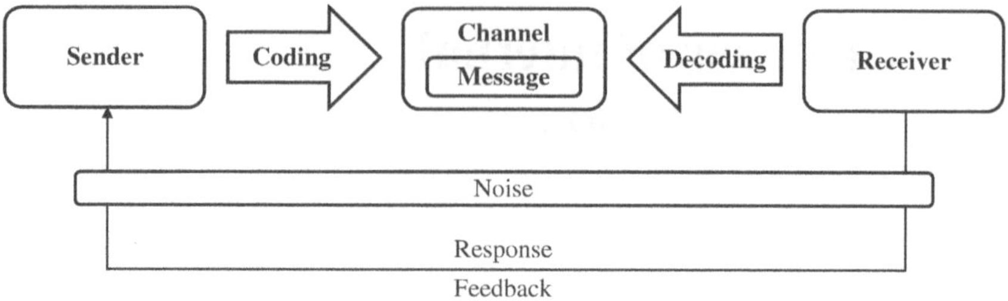

Figure 4.1 Model of the communication process within organizations. The model was developed in a general form by Shannon and Weaver (1950) and adapted by Harrison (1995) to the organizational context.

Internal communication channels

Internal communication channels can be simplistically divided into what we term "traditional" (analog) or "new" (online, digital), though other authors name these categories somewhat differently (e.g. Cresenzo, 2011; Holtz, 2004; Wright & Robertson, 2009; Yue et al., 2021)

Traditional internal communication channels

Newsletters, once much more popular than today (Wright & Robertson, 2009), remain a valuable internal communication channel. They allow organizations to reach all their employees with a consistent message (FitzPatrick & Valskov, 2014). Newsletters are best used for transmitting short messages (Holtz, 2004) and are the best way to reach remote employees or employees who lack access to other channels (FitzPatrick & Valskov, 2014; Holtz, 2004; Wright & Robertson, 2009). Magazines, another internal communication channel, are similar to newsletters but tend to be more detailed and less frequent (Holtz, 2004). Information boards are a good medium to share instructions and brief information (FitzPatrick & Valskov, 2014), but they are often ignored (Wright & Robertson, 2009). Posters are a more attention-grabbing medium because they can be hung in unusual, unexpected places, while performing the same function as information boards (Holtz, 2004; Wright & Robertson, 2009). All these channels are print channels, which some have called redundant (Cresenzo, 2011), yet which have the advantage of being portable and capable of reaching all employees (Holtz, 2004; Smith & Mounter, 2008). Thus, print channels can play a supporting role in internal communication processes, such as by transmitting additional information, ultimately strengthening employees' identification with the organization (Cresenzo, 2011; Smith & Mounter, 2008).

Another traditional internal communication channel is face-to-face communication, which occurs between two people (one-on-one) or among a group (Smith & Mounter, 2008). Such communication is effective at "conveying complex, nonroutine messages and facilitating immediate feedback" (Yue et al., 2021, p. 27). It is particularly important within organizations because it often increases employee satisfaction (Men, 2014a; Tkalac Verčič & Špoljarić, 2020), leading to greater commitment to the organization (Wolfeld, 2010); it strengthens engagement (Men, 2014b); and it solidifies relationships among employees (Lee, 2010; O'Kane & Hargie, 2007). These benefits reflect the fact that face-to-face communication offers features that other forms of communication do not. Face-to-face communication involves verbal and non-verbal cues, such as tone of voice, facial expressions and body language (Holtz, 2004), which enables managers to transfer and interpret social and emotional cues (Men, 2014a, 2014b). This channel can be exploited by managers to build relationships with employees (Lee, 2010), and it can strengthen relationships among colleagues. However, despite its many benefits, face-to-face communication is being used less frequently due to the availability of digital communication channels. These new channels allow delivery of one message in the same way to every receiver, which is impossible with face-to-face communication. On the other hand, face-to-face communication creates a connection between sender and receiver that can engender trust, something digital channels struggle to achieve (Holtz, 2004).

New internal communication channels

New internal communication channels are essentially all channels that require the use of technology. Wright and Robertson (2009) divide them into media-based (electronic) and web-enabled (online). Most electronic channels are digitized forms of print channels, with the notable exceptions of video and telephone. Online channels try to mimic face-to-face communication in different ways (Tsai & Men, 2017) by virtue of their interactivity (Yue et al., 2021). In fact, interactivity is being added whenever possible to electronic channels, turning them into online channels (Cresenzo, 2011). While interactivity brings these channels closer to face-to-face communication, they are not necessarily the same: feedback is nearly instantaneous in face-to-face interactions (Nohria & Eccles, 2000), but not in all online channels. On the other hand, online channels can bridge tremendous physical distance between people, which would otherwise make face-to-face communication impossible or at least impractical (Asheim et al., 2007). Online channels have gained in importance since 2020, when the COVID-19 pandemic changed the way organizations operate. Remote work requires employers to be able to reach their employees at home, and vice versa. This massive shift from face-to-face toward online communication has compromised some aspects of organizations but potentiated others (Tkalac Verčič et al., 2021).

Most recently, organizations have begun to use internal social networks more frequently as a result of technological advances (Cresenzo, 2011), mirroring a similar communication trend in society in general

(Leonardi et al., 2013; Men et al., 2020). In fact, Leonardi et al. (2013) have described an all-encompassing channel that they named *enterprise social media platform* and defined as "web-based platforms that allow workers to (1) communicate messages with specific co-workers or broadcast messages to everyone in the organization; (2) explicitly indicate or implicitly reveal particular coworkers as communication partners; (3) post, edit, and sort text and files linked to themselves or others; and (4) view the messages, connections, text, and files communicated, posted, edited and sorted by anyone else in the organization at any time of their choosing" (p. 2). Treem and Leonardi (2012) noted that, in the context of internal communication, social media provide visibility, ensure perseverance, enable content editability, and encourage relationships and connections, which they predicted might "alter socialization, information sharing, and power processes in organizations" (p. 143). These far-reaching consequences that they predicted a decade ago seem to have come true with the changes catalyzed by the COVID-19 pandemic (Tkalac Verčič et al., 2021). Internal social media owe their importance to the many advantages they bring to organizations: they increase social capital (King & Lee, 2016), thereby strengthening organizational identity (Martin et al., 2011), knowledge sharing (Jarrahi, 2017), decision-making (Madsen & Johansen, 2019), and employee engagement (Men et al., 2020).

Media richness theory

The effectiveness of internal communication channels is discussed most often in terms of media richness theory, which was developed in 1984 by Daft and Lengel (Tkalac Verčič & Špoljarić, 2020). Media richness theory holds that internal communication messages should be delivered through channels that provide a message-appropriate level of information richness in order to remove any confusion and ambiguity. The theory defines information richness as the capacity of a channel to deliver potential information (Daft & Lengel, 1984). In other words, channels used for internal communication need to meet the requirements of the message they are supposed to deliver (Trevino et al., 1987). Whether a channel can deliver the information in the message refers to whether it can provide immediate or at least rapid feedback; multiple cues, such as verbal and non-verbal; variations in language; and personalization (Daft & Lengel, 1984, 1986). Thus, channels run the spectrum from rich to lean, with moderate media channels in between (Daft & Lengel, 1986). The rule of thumb is that the lower the chance of confusion, the leaner the channel can – and should – be (Wright & Robertson, 2009). Thus, channels that are of lower richness are used for unequivocal messages, while richer channels are used for messages that require immediate feedback in order to reduce ambiguity (Daft & Lengel, 1984, 1986). However, Dennis and Kinney (1998) argue that the richness of a channel does not necessarily have a significant impact on its ability to transfer information of certain richness. They point out that media richness theory applies well to traditional channels, but not entirely to new channels. This is because digital channels are much more adaptable than traditional ones (Pagani, 2000), and their level of interactivity can be adjusted if necessary.

Categorization of internal communication channels

The considerable differences between traditional and new channels make relevant Berger's (2008) categorization of the two types of channels into print, interpersonal (oral) and electronic channels. This categorization does not start from media richness theory, but rather focuses on the method of message delivery. Inspired by this, we argue for a categorization of electronic channels that includes an additional category, interpersonal electronic channels. This leads us to propose a matrix of internal communication channels based on levels of digitalization and interactivity (Table 4.1). This approach categorizes internal communication channels while taking into account the method of delivery and media richness theory.

Choosing internal communication channels

The choice of channel for internal communication affects the end result of the entire communication process (FitzPatrick & Valskov, 2014), which can be considered effective if the relevant message is sent through adequate channels (Tkalac Verčič & Špoljarić, 2020). No channel provides a

Table 4.1 Matrix of traditional and new internal communication channels

	Traditional	*New*
Not interactive	Newsletters Magazines Information boards Posters Memos Mail sent to home	Digital newsletters Information on LCD or other screens Podcasts Blogs Video posts Group e-mails
Somewhat interactive	Meetings in larger groups Live events	Intranet One-on-one e-mails Live web-casting Video conferencing in larger groups Social networks Internal communication applications (apps)
Interactive	Meetings in smaller groups Team building One-on-one interactions Rumor mills	Video conferencing in smaller groups One-on-one video conferencing

"one-size-fits-all" solution. Choosing adequate channels means considering employees' needs and wants (Tkalac Verčič & Špoljarić, 2020; Welch, 2011; Wood, 1999). As Tkalac Verčič (2021) put it, "in various situations, certain channels are more appropriate than others" (p. 246).

Numerous factors determine the choice of internal communication channels, including organizational profile, size, and culture, as well as the cultural background of the employees (Dévényi, 2016). We argue that even more important are the receiver's characteristics, needs and wants; as well as the desired outcomes of the internal communication, as FitzPatrick and Valskov (2014) rightly emphasize. The appropriate mix of channels depends on whether the primary goals are, for example, to foster employee satisfaction, engagement, organizational identification and understanding; or to communicate change. Choosing the right mix of internal communication channels can strongly affect the final outcome because "how you say something is often as important as what you say" (FitzPatrick & Valskov, 2014, p. 92). This led Quirke (1996, 2017) to introduce the idea of the "channels escalator", which draws on media richness theory to stipulate that the desired outcomes of internal communication should match the level of richness a channel offers. The channels escalator stratifies channels by the desired level of involvement and matches them to the degree of change being communicated. The designed involvement can range from minimal to maximal in the trend: awareness < understanding < support < involvement < commitment (Quirke, 2017). If the desired outcome is simply awareness, the internal communication channel mix should consist of lean media channels. At the other extreme, if the desired communication outcome is employee commitment, rich media channels should be used. Intermediate levels of involvement call for a mix of lean, moderate, and rich media channels.

As part of the research project from which this book emerged, we examined how often organizations in Croatia used different internal communication channels. During four years, we conducted qualitative and quantitative research in 26 organizations, comprising 14 branches of international organizations, 3 domestic-based multinational organizations, 5 domestic organizations, and 4 state-owned organizations. Data were collected in two phases: the first phase began in May 2019 and ended in October 2019, while the second phase began in October 2020 and lasted until February 2021. This means that our data were collected before the COVID-19 pandemic and during its first wave. The dataset from the first phase included 1,805 employees from 12 organizations; the data from the second phase, 1,652 employees from the other 14 organizations. At each organization, we first interviewed directors of corporate communications and human resources management in order to find out about internal communication practices. After their interview, the directors were asked to fill out a questionnaire about which channels were used for internal communication and how often (daily, weekly, monthly, occasionally, never). (The questionnaire is shown in Table 5.3.) Participants from the first 12 organizations filled out

Table 4.2 Internal communication channels used before and during the COVID-19 pandemic in 14 Croatian organizations (second phase of the research project)

	Pre-Pandemic	*During the Pandemic*
Rich Media		
Video chats	7	11
Team building meetings	14	4
Other meetings	6	3
Moderate Media		
Town hall meetings	13	7
Blogs	6	7
Corporate social networks	8	10
Specially developed applications for internal communication	6	11
Planned, formal discussions with top management	11	9
Intranet	13	13
Educational meetings	13	12
Lean Media		
Digital newsletters	3	5
Printed newsletters	2	2
Group e-mails	14	14
Meetings (all employees)	11	6
Memos and mail (within organization)	8	8
Mail sent to home	8	10
Information boards	12	11
Posters	10	10
Information on LCD or other screens	8	7

the questionnaire only once. However, the participants from the remaining 14 organizations filled it out twice, on the same occasion: once with reference to what channels were used before the pandemic, and once with reference to what channels they were using currently, i.e. during the pandemic. In this way, we wanted to analyze how the pandemic was changing the mix of internal communication channels (Table 4.2).

As expected, the COVID-19 pandemic led organizations to use video chats and different types of social networks more often, while meetings involving many employees became less frequent. This reflects the global shift toward remote working (Ernstsson & Hållén, 2021).

We also wanted to examine whether the choice of internal communication channels affected internal communication satisfaction in our sample of organizations. After all, certain channels are more effective than others for transferring certain types of messages. Employees usually prefer general information to be delivered through lean media, but they desire a certain level of interactivity when receiving more personal information, which requires rich media (Byrne & LeMay, 2006). We found that all media channels significantly impacted internal communication satisfaction, except town hall meetings, blogs, printed newsletters and mail sent to home (Table 4.3). Internal communication satisfaction

Table 4.3 Impact of specific internal communication channels on internal communication satisfaction

	Use	*N (org.)*	*M*	*SD*	*t-test*	*df*	*Asymp.Sig. (2-Tailed)*
Rich Media							
Video chats	No	7	4.12	1.27	−12.143	3,451	.000*
	Yes	19	4.70	1.30			
Team building meetings	No	11	4.39	1.39	−5.613	3,451	.000*
	Yes	15	4.64	1.24			
Other meetings	No	17	4.45	1.35	−4.179	3,451	.000*
	Yes	9	4.65	1.25			
Moderate Media							
Town hall meetings	No	8	4.65	1.37	3.457	3,451	.001
	Yes	18	4.48	1.29			
Blogs	No	14	4.54	1.31	.709	3,451	.478
	Yes	12	4.51	1.32			
Corporate social networks	No	9	4.32	1.34	−7.510	3,451	.000*
	Yes	17	4.66	1.28			
Specially developed applications for internal communication	No	9	4.29	1.26	−9.334	3,451	.000*
	Yes	17	4.70	1.33			
Planned, formal discussions with top management	No	7	4.73	1.31	4.972	3,451	.000*
	Yes	19	4.46	1.30			
Intranet	No	1	6.10	.65	7.167	3,451	.000*
	Yes	25	4.51	1.31			
Educational meetings	No	2	5.21	1.19	7.689	3,451	.000*
	Yes	24	4.48	1.31			
Lean Media							
Digital newsletters	No	13	4.45	1.37	−3.743	3,451	.000*
	Yes	13	4.62	1.25			
Printed newsletters	No	17	4.58	1.36	3.075	3,451	.002
	Yes	9	4.44	1.24			
Meetings (all employees)	No	11	4.62	1.31	3.650	3,451	.000*
	Yes	15	4.45	1.32			
Memos and mail (within organization)	No	10	4.73	1.32	6.010	3,451	.000*
	Yes	16	4.44	1.30			
Mail sent to home	No	10	4.57	1.32	1.494	3,451	.135
	Yes	16	4.50	1.31			
Information boards	No	6	4.77	1.32	4.879	3,451	.000*
	Yes	20	4.48	1.31			
Posters	No	5	4.85	1.42	6.156	3,451	.000*
	Yes	21	4.47	1.29			
Information on LCD or other screens	No	11	4.40	1.39	−4.720	3,451	.000*
	Yes	15	4.62	1.25			

Note: Group e-mails were used in all 26 organizations; intranet, in 25.

* $p < .001$.

was uniformly high in organizations that used rich media, but the situation was more complex in organizations using moderate and lean media. Certain moderate and lean media were associated with higher internal communication satisfaction than other media. Nevertheless, one clear trend emerged: the moderate and lean media associated with higher internal communication satisfaction were digital, while those associated with lower satisfaction were not digital and involved minimal or no interactivity.

Conclusion

Internal communication channels are the medium through which messages within organizations are delivered. Even though management is most often the sender of such messages, some internal communication channels allow for two-way communication. Such communication channels are considered rich by media richness theory, meaning that they enable interaction with immediate feedback. Rich traditional channels usually include face-to-face communication, but some digital channels can also be considered rich. At the other extreme are lean media channels, such as print channels and their digital versions, such as digital information boards, newsletters, blogs, and video posts. However, different types of messages and desired communication outcomes require different levels of media richness. As a result, internal communication practitioners have to determine the appropriate level of media richness for the specific message they want to deliver. Once the level of media richness has been determined, internal communication practitioners should also consider employees that they are supposed to reach in order to formulate the best mix of channels for broadcasting the message within the organization. For this, there is no "one-size-fits-all" solution.

References

Asheim, B., Coenen, L., & Vang, J. (2007). Face-to-face, buzz, and knowledge bases: Sociospatial implications for learning, innovation, and innovation policy. *Environment and Planning C: Government and Policy*, *25*(5), 655–670. https://doi.org/10.1068/c0648

Berger, B. (2008, November 17). *Employee/organizational communications*. Institute for Public Relations. https://instituteforpr.org/employee-organizational-communications/

Byrne, Z. S., & LeMay, E. (2006). Different media for organizational communication: Perceptions of quality and satisfaction. *Journal of Business and Psychology*, *21*(2), 149–173. https://doi.org/10.1007/s10869-006-9023-8

Cresenzo, S. (2011). Integrating employee communications media. In T. L. Gillis (Ed.), *The IABC handbook of organizational communication* (2nd ed., pp. 2019–2230). Josey-Bass.

Daft, R. L., & Lengel, R. H. (1984). Information richness: A new approach to managerial behavior and organizational design. *Research in Organizational Behavior*, *6*, 191–233.

Daft, R. L., & Lengel, R. H. (1986). Organizational information requirements, media richness and structural design. *Management Science*, *32*(5), 554–571.

Dennis, A. R., & Kinney, S. T. (1998). Testing media richness theory in the new media: The effects of cues, feedback, and task equivocality. *Information Systems Research*, *9*(3), 256–274. https://doi.org/10.1287/isre.9.3.256

Dévényi, M. (2016). The role of integrative strategies and tactics in HR negotiations. *Strategic Management*, *21*(2), 32–36.

Ernstsson, H., & Hållén, F. (2021). *"All That Is Solid Melts Into Virtual Work": A study of the implications of the Covid-19 pandemic on contemporary Employer Branding through the lens of Social Acceleration* [Bachelor's Thesis, Lund University]. https://lup.lub.lu.se/student-papers/search/publication/9048348

Fawkes, J. (2012). Public relations and communications. In A. Theaker (Ed.), *The public relations handbook* (4th ed., pp. 21–37). Routledge.

FitzPatrick, L., & Valskov, K. (2014). *Internal communications: A manual for practitioners*. Kogan Page.

Harrison, S. (1995). *Public relations – An introduction*. International Thomson Business Press.

Holtz, S. (2004). *Corporate conversations: A guide to crafting effective and appropriate internal communications*. American Management Association.

Jarrahi, M. H. (2017). Social media, social capital, and knowledge sharing in enterprise. *IT Professional*, *20*(4), 37–45. https://doi.org/10.1109/MITP.2017.265105759

King, C., & Lee, H. (2016). Enhancing internal communication to build social capital amongst hospitality employees – The role of social media. *International Journal of Contemporary Hospitality Management*, *28*(12), 2675–2695. https://doi.org/10.1108/IJCHM-06-2015-0321

Lee, C. E. (2010). Face-to-face versus computer-mediated communication: Exploring employees' preference of effective employee communication channel. *International Journal for the Advancement of Science & Arts*, *1*(2), 38–48.

Leonardi, P. M., Huysman, M., & Steinfield, C. (2013). Enterprise social media: Definition, history, and prospects for the study of social technologies in organizations. *Journal of Computer-Mediated Communication*, *19*(1), 1–19. https://doi.org/10.1111/jcc4.12029

Madsen, V. T., & Johansen, W. (2019). A spiral of voice? When employees speak up on internal social media. *Journal of Communication Management*, *23*(4), 331–347. https://doi.org/10.1108/JCOM-03-2019-0050

Martin, G., Gollan, P. J., & Grigg, K. (2011). Is there a bigger and better future for employer branding? Facing up to innovation, corporate reputations and wicked problems in SHRM. *The International Journal of Human Resource Management*, *22*(17), 3618–3637. https://doi.org/10.1080/09585192.2011.560880

Men, L. R. (2014a). Strategic internal communication: Transformational leadership, communication channels, and employee satisfaction. *Management Communication Quarterly*, *28*(2), 264–284. https://doi.org/10.1177/0893318914524536

Men, L. R. (2014b). Why leadership matters to internal communication: Linking transformational leadership, symmetrical communication, and employee outcomes. *Journal of Public Relations Research*, *26*(3), 256–279. https://doi.org/10.1080/1062726X.2014.908719

Men, L. R., O'Neil, J., & Ewing, M. (2020). Examining the effects of internal social media on employee engagement. *Public Relations Review*, *46*(2). https://doi.org/10.1016/j.pubrev.2020.101880

Nohria, N., & Eccles, R. (2000). Face-to-face: Making network organizations work. In P. Dawson, I. MacLouglin, & D. Preece (Eds.), *Technology, organizations and innovation: Critical perspectives on business and management* (pp. 1659–1681). Routledge.

O'Kane, P., & Hargie, O. (2007). Intentional and unintentional consequences of substituting face-to-face interaction with e-mail: An employee-based perspective. *Interacting with Computers*, *19*(1), 20–31. https://doi.org/10.1016/j.intcom.2006.07.008

Pagani, M. (2000). *Multimedia and interactive digital TV: Managing the opportunities created by digital convergence: Managing the opportunities created by digital convergence*. IRM Press.

Quirke, B. (1996). *Communicating corporate change: A practical guide to communication and corporate strategy*. McGraw-Hill.

Quirke, B. (2017). *Making the connections: Using internal communication to turn strategy into action* (2nd ed.). Routledge.

Shannon, C. E., & Weaver, W. (1949). *The mathematical theory of communication*. The University of Illinois Press.

Smith, L., & Mounter, P. (2008). *Effective internal communication* (2nd ed.). Kogan Page Publishers.

Tkalac Verčič, A. (2016). *Odnosi s javnošću*. PRint.

Tkalac Verčič, A. (2021). Closing thoughts and future directions. In L. R. Men, & A. T. Verčič (Eds.), *Current trends and issues in internal communication: Theory and practice* (pp. 241–258). Palgrave Macmillan.

Tkalac Verčič, A., & Špoljarić, A. (2020). Managing internal communication: How the choice of channels affects internal communication satisfaction. *Public Relations Review*, *46*(3), 101926. https://doi.org/10.1016/j.pubrev.2020.101926

Tkalac Verčič, A., Verčič, D., & Špoljarić, A. (2021). *The effect of Covid on internal communication channel preference* [Conference presentation]. BledCom 2021, Bled, Slovenia.

Treem, J. W., & Leonardi, P. M. (2012). Social media use in organizations: Exploring the affordances of visibility, editability, persistence, and association. In C. T. Salomn (Ed.), *Communication yearbook* (Vol. 36, pp. 143–189). Routledge.

Trevino, L. K., Lengel, R. H., & Daft, R. L. (1987). Media symbolism, media richness, and media choice in organizations: A symbolic interactionist perspective. *Communication Research*, *14*(5), 553–574. https://doi.org/10.1177/009365087014005006

Tsai, W. H. S., & Men, L. R. (2017). Social CEOs: The effects of CEOs' communication styles and parasocial interaction on social networking sites. *New media & Society*, *19*(11), 1848–1867. https://doi.org/10.1177/1461444816643922

Welch, M. (2011). The evolution of the employee engagement concept: Communication implications. *Corporate Communications: An International Journal*, *16*(4), 328–346. https://doi.org/10.1108/13563281111186968

Wolfeld, L. R. (2010). Effects of office layout on job satisfaction, productivity and organizational commitment as transmitted through face-to-face interactions. *Colonial Academic Alliance Undergraduate Research Journal*, *1*(1), 8.

Wood, J. (1999). Establishing internal communication channels that work. *Journal of Higher Education Policy and Management*, *21*(2), 135–149.

Wright, M., & Robertson, F. (2009). Creating an internal communication strategy. In M. Wright (Ed.), *Gower handbook of internal communication* (2nd ed., pp. 19–48). Gower Publishing.

Yue, C. A., Men, L. R., & Berger, B. K. (2021). Leaders as communication agents. In L. R. Men, & A. T. Verčič (Eds.), *Current trends and issues in internal communication: Theory and practice* (pp. 19–38). Palgrave Macmillan.

5 Evaluating internal communication

Internal communication makes use of various strategies and tactics (Tkalac Verčič, 2021), but its success can be measured only if appropriate metrics are used (Men & Bowen, 2017). Why measure the effectiveness of internal communication? Good communication within organizations, and between organizations and external stakeholders, brings numerous benefits: a healthy internal atmosphere, teamwork as the norm, satisfied employees and customers, greater productivity and innovation, and sustainable competitive advantage. Extensive evidence links effective internal communication to positive outcomes, including organizational success (Robson & Tourish, 2005); organizational efficiency (Quinn & Hargie, 2004); higher productivity, lower absenteeism, higher quality of services and products, greater innovation, fewer strikes, and lower operating costs (Clampitt & Downs, 1993); employee trust (Men et al., 2020); employee advocacy (Men, 2014a); organizational reputation (Men, 2014b); organizational citizenship behavior (Men & Yue, 2019); and work-life enrichment (Jiang & Men, 2017). Conversely, poor internal communication can have many negative consequences, such as feelings of isolation and dissatisfaction, lower levels of involvement in decision-making processes, insecurity, and increased employee alienation (Hargie & Tourish, 2000).

As the theory and practice of internal communication have matured, different approaches for measuring its effectiveness have been used. The question for an organization remains: what variables to measure? Only when that question has been answered, can we move on to how to measure them.

Internal communication audits

Grunig and Hunt (1984) suggested measuring retention of key organizational messages by employees, an approach that Tourish and Hargie (2009) term managerial, because it is based on the role of communication as delivering messages to employees "so that everyone can sign up for the vision and direction set by the top management team" (p. 5). In this approach, the effectiveness of internal communication can be measured through communication audits, co-orientational analyses, internal

DOI: 10.4324/9781003200109-5

communication satisfaction surveys and communication network analyses. A more nuanced approach divides the evaluation of internal communication into the measurement of outputs, outtakes, and outcomes (Broom & Dozier, 1990; Lindenmann, 1993; Men & Bowen, 2017). We favor this nuanced approach because it measures communication by taking into account the complex realities and meanings that employees attach to specific phenomena (Tourish & Hargie, 2009).

To acquire accurate information on how key internal publics perceive communication, the most appropriate approach is to determine employees' attitudes toward the organization (Argenti, 2007). This can be accomplished through a communication audit (Tourish & Hargie, 2009), which has been used extensively in public relations (Kopec, 1982), human resources management (Dickson et al., 2003; Varona, 1996), strategic marketing (Stone, 1995), and other business areas (Gray & Laidlaw, 2004). Kopec defined a communication audit as a "complete analysis of an organization's communications, internal and/or external, designed to 'take a picture' of communication needs, policies, practices, and capabilities and to uncover necessary data to allow top management to make informed, economical decisions about future objectives of the organization's communication" (1982, p. 24). According to Dickson et al. (2003) an audit is essentially an evaluation of a certain process. Historically, audits were performed to assess the financial health of an organization, but this concept of systematically scrutinizing the performance of corporate systems and strategies has entered the field of communication. The main goal of an audit is to put people's interactions into the context of a complex set of relationships that the participants may perceive in different ways. In other words, a communication audit "takes a communication perspective on the organization" (Downs & Adrian, 2004, p. 6). Audits can include and combine different methodologies, most of which originated in social sciences. Below we describe the methods that we used in the research project from which this book emerged.

Methodologies for evaluation

Interviews: general considerations

The interview is a first step and central tool in many different types of research, and evaluation of internal communication is no exception. A series of interviews served as our starting point for the project presented in this book. Downs (1988) concluded that if you can use only one methodology, choose the interview. Even though we may not recommend this advice in all situations, interviews do have certain advantages that make them nearly obligatory for any evaluation.

Perhaps the most powerful unique feature of an interview is its social nature. It allows a personal, direct approach to measurement and can be conducted in different ways, whether face-to-face, by telephone or via electronic channels. Interviews allow a larger number of questions, which can be open-ended or closed, and their order does not necessarily need to be set. They can be the first step in quantitative research, especially if we construct our own instruments. They can also be the final step in such research, in order to understand the data better (Tkalac Verčič et al., 2009). Interviews are more likely to elicit unanticipated responses and provide depth and meaning to acquired quantitative information (Forman & Argenti, 2005). They bring a human and social dimension to the analysis of an organization, and they help researchers get a better sense of organizational practices and potential problems as interpreted by different employees (Millar & Tracey, 2009).

Interviews vary depending on the level of formality or structure and can generally be classified as structured, semi-structured, or unstructured. Structured interviews are standardized, which means in practice that questionnaires are used to collect data from employees. Semi-structured and unstructured questionnaires are usually not standardized, which means that the researcher brings pre-prepared questions that serve as a framework of the topics to be covered but that can be adjusted and that give the employee freedom in responding (Tkalac Verčič et al., 2009). Rarely, questionnaires are standardized, meaning that in all interviews, the questions are discussed in the same way and in the same sequence.

Planning an interview requires detailed analysis of the primary and secondary literature. Then researchers formulate an interview outline covering the major topics and questions to be discussed. It is best to pre-test the questions to ensure that they are understandable. The interviewer attempts to obtain detailed, in-depth answers. Employees can be completely free in how they answer, and it is the interviewer's job to adjust to the interviewee and his or her way of communicating, while still steering the conversation in the pre-designed direction. In certain cases, some questions can be personalized, which requires an experienced interviewer. In fact, interviewers should have well developed skills in order to increase the validity of the data from the interview (Millar & Tracey, 2009).

The choice of interviewee is quite important. When working with respondents who are employees of formal organizations, it is necessary to go through formal gatekeepers (Seidman, 1998).

Interviews: our research

In our project we used the face-to-face approach for the first 34 interviews and, due to the COVID-19 pandemic, video conferencing for the other 26 interviews. We used the semi-structured, non-standardized approach to explore five major topics (Table 5.1).

Our interviews lasted between 35 and 55 minutes, depending on the respondent. We taped entire interviews, after asking the respondents for

Table 5.1 Interview questions for mapping internal communication in an organization

1 What does internal communication include?

- a What does internal communication in your organization include?
- b Where is internal communication in your organization positioned?
- c How many people in your organization are employed in internal communication?
- d Who oversees internal communication in your organization?
- e What types of tasks are a part of the internal communication function?
- f Who oversees employer branding (if anyone)?
- g Who oversees employee engagement (if anyone)?
- h What types of tasks are included in employer branding and employee engagement?
- i What type of cooperation is there between the corporate communication and human resource departments?
- j Are you satisfied with how the responsibilities are divided between the two departments?

2 Internal communication channels

- a What are the major communication channels in your organization?
- b Which channels do you use (intranet, electronic mail, face-to-face meetings...)?
- c Are there differences among employees in their channel preferences (according to age, type of employee, subject...)?

3 Internal communication measurement

- a Do you use any kind of evaluation in internal communication (including employer branding, employee engagement, reputation)?
- b What do you measure and how often?
- c What kind of change is implemented based on the evaluation results?

4 Consequences of internal communication for organizational success

- a What do you see as consequences of good or bad internal communication for your organization?
- b Could you give us an example of when good or bad internal communication had certain consequences?

5 The future of internal communication

- a What do you see as the major focus of internal communication in the future?
- b How do you see future development in this area (with emphasis on employer branding and employee engagement)?

their consent. All responses were then transcribed and analyzed. The initial questions were the same for heads of corporate communications and human resources, since one of our goals was to determine whether the two directors view the internal communication function differently. Some of the main conclusions are described below.

None of the organizations had a separate internal communication department or a person specifically in charge of internal communication. In most organizations, internal communication was the responsibility of one or a few employees in corporate communications. In some cases when there was no corporate communication department, marketing staff handled internal communication tasks.

Most interviewees, whether in corporate communications or human resources, agreed that internal communication involves transferring information within organizations. However, there was no clear agreement on the direction of transfer. Most respondents, especially those from human resources, saw it as one-way communication with the main goal of informing employees. Typically, they saw it as a process in which management sends information and employees receive it. Only a handful of respondents expressed a wider view of communication as a two-way, symmetrical process.

Most organizations relied on e-mail as an internal communication channel, even though almost all respondents complained about email overflow. All organizations used intranet in some form or another, but with very different approaches. In organizations where intranet was seen as a medium for two-way communication, it was much more popular among employees than other channels. In organizations where the intranet was not managed by an official "editor", employees could find it confusing and either overloaded or deficient in information. All the largest organizations in our sample used social media such as Workplace, but with varying degrees of success and employee satisfaction. All organizations, regardless of size, had workplace bulletin boards, but they were far more important in manufacturing firms, in which large groups of employees did not have access to internet. Many organizations had newsletters, usually digital, yet they did not seem to be popular among employees.

All our interviewees, whether from corporate communication or human resources, showed strong interest in employer branding and stated that it was important for their organizations. However, most did not conduct organized activities to promote it. Most organizations, especially multinational ones, monitored employee engagement yet did not do much with the results. Some organizations conducted employee research using, for examples, indices of performance enablement, engagement, inclusion, and diversity; but it was unclear whether they modified their strategies based on the results.

All our respondents agreed that internal communication was important for organizational success. Most emphasized transparent and timely communication as factors important for successful internal communication. All interviewees in the second phase of our project, during the COVID-19 pandemic, agreed that frequent, extensive internal communication, together with moral support, led to very good results and helped employees maintain a positive attitude. They stated that internal communication was key for keeping the challenging situation under control. All respondents indicated their belief that the future would bring even greater digitalization of internal communication.

In starting our research project with interviews, we recognized the "richness and authenticity of narratives and stories as a major source of information about organization" (Millar & Tracey, 2009, p. 102). The next steps of our project were based on our ability to listen, understand, and analyze what our respondents told us.

Questionnaires: general considerations

Questionnaires, often called instruments although the two terms are not interchangeable, are the most important method for measuring employees' attitudes and perceptions. Relatively few routinely used instruments exist for evaluating organizational communications. Downs et al. (1994) have classified these instruments into three categories: comprehensive, communication process, or organizational outcomes. Comprehensive instruments analyze communicational practices on a macro level and include instruments such as the International Communication Association Audit, the Organizational Communication Scale, and the Communication Satisfaction Questionnaire. Communication process instruments focus on analyzing facets of organizational communication rather than gaining a comprehensive view of it. Areas commonly covered include conflict, mentoring, competence, and management communication. The third category of instruments focuses on organizational outcomes such as satisfaction, productivity, and commitment; examples are the Communications Satisfaction Questionnaire and the Organization Identification Questionnaire. Below we briefly describe some of the instruments.

Roberts and O'Reilly developed the Organizational Communication Scale (OCS) in 1974 to measure "communication variables in organizations". The OCS is composed of 35 items measuring 16 dimensions of organizational communication (DeWine, 1994). The two investigators then used the instrument to measure differences in communication behavior between members of organizations who isolate (so called isolates) or who participate (so called participants) in communication (DeWine, 1994). Various subscales allowed them to conclude that isolates sometimes deliberately withheld information, while participants were associated with perceptions of increased information and greater overall satisfaction with communication.

The Communication Satisfaction Questionnaire (CSQ) was developed by Downs and Hazen (1977) to analyze the relationship between communication and job satisfaction. The questionnaire of 88 items was based mostly on literature reviews and interviews, and it was administered to 225 employees with various demographic characteristics. Although developed more than 25 years ago, the CSQ remains the dominant measure of communication satisfaction in applied and basic research. The eight CSQ factors are Communication Climate, Supervisory Communication, Organizational Integration, Media Quality, Co-worker

Communication, Corporate Information, Personal Feedback, and Subordinate Communication.

From 1971 to 1976, the Organizational Communication Division of the International Communication Association (ICA) developed a package of instruments to assess organizational communication and employees' perceptions of communication processes in their organizations (Downs & Adrian, 2004; Hargie & Tourish, 2000). The objective of the ICA Audit was to develop standardized procedures for assessing communication, but also to establish a normed data bank that would enable comparisons among different organizations (Goldhaber, 2002). The total assessment package included a standardized survey questionnaire, interview guides, observations, network analysis, critical incidents, and a communication diary (Downs & Adrian, 2004).

The Organizational Communication Development Audit system was developed by Wiio and colleagues at the Helsinki Research Institute for Business Economics during their research of more than 200 European organizations (Greenbaum et al., 1988). The instrument was designed to determine whether and how an organization's internal communication system helps it translate its goals into results. The original objectives of the instrument were to measure the communication climate, defined as the perceived atmosphere of opinions and attitudes; assess communication satisfaction and job satisfaction; identify possible bottlenecks in organizational communication; and enable comparisons between organizations (Downs et al., 1994) quickly and inexpensively.

Given that most instruments for assessing communication satisfaction and organizational communication were designed and validated in the US (Yamaguchi, 2017), we were motivated a decade ago to construct an instrument that would update dimensions of internal communication satisfaction and be adapted to the Croatian, and by extension European, setting. We also wanted an instrument that would provide better understanding of how employees judge various aspects of an organization's communication system. Thus, we developed the Questionnaire for Measuring Internal Communication Satisfaction (*Upitnik za mjerenje zadovoljstva internom komunikacijom*, UPZIK) (Tkalac Verčič et al., 2009) based on the approach of Downs and Hazen (1977). The UPZIK focuses on employee attitudes and perceptions of different communication practices. In the first stage of UPZIK development, the initial questionnaire of 107 items was administered to 259 employees, after which the factors were analyzed, and the survey was reduced to 8 dimensions and 32 items. Items asked about interpersonal communication, organizational climate, and communication with the supervisor, and some items were absent from other instruments, including items about satisfaction with internal communication channels and digital media. In the second stage of UPZIK development, the new questionnaire was administered to 225 employees in two large organizations. Based on the results, the questionnaire was factor-analyzed a second time and found to correlate with job satisfaction. In fact, the instrument was found to be reliable, valid, and applicable for future theoretical and practical research. Since its development, the UPZIK has been applied in numerous studies (Borovec & Balgač, 2017; Lalić et al., 2012; Pološki Vokić et al., 2020; Sinčić Ćorić et al., 2020; Tkalac Verčič & Pološki Vokić, 2017; Tkalac Verčič & Špoljarić, 2020), and it has performed reliably and proven easy to administer.

In the final version of the UPZIK, employees assess their satisfaction on Likert-type scales ranging from 1 ("extremely dissatisfied") to 7 ("extremely satisfied"). For example, two items are "Satisfaction with the outcomes of communicating with colleagues" and "Satisfaction with information on work protocols". The complete instrument includes four other scales used to measure employee engagement, perceived organizational support (POS), psychological contract fulfillment, and employer attractiveness. Confirmatory factor analysis of the UPZIK tested the validity of the second-order factorial structure. The resulting model had eight domains as first-order internal communication satisfaction factors, and one second-order factor that represented general satisfaction with internal communication in organization.

Employee engagement has been defined as a fulfilling work-related state of mind characterized by vigor, dedication, and absorption (Schaufeli et al., 2002) and measured using the Utrecht Work Engagement Scale (UWES). This scale was developed for measuring engagement with work, and it includes three dimensions. Employees assess their engagement on Likert-type scales ranging from 1 ("never") to 7 ("always"), and examples of items include "At my work, I feel bursting with energy" and "I am enthusiastic about my job". The UWES has been used and validated multiple times (Bakker & Demerouti, 2008). Despite its extensive use, it remains unclear whether the concept is multidimensional; two studies have suggested it to have a three-dimensional structure (Hallberg & Schaufeli, 2006; Schaufeli & Bakker, 2004).

POS has been defined as a measure of general belief held by the employee that the organization is committed to them, values their involvement, and has concern for their well-being and evaluated using a scale developed by Eisenberger et al. (1986). Using a Likert-type scale ranging from 1 to 7, employees indicate their agreement with statements such as "the organization values my contribution to its well-being" and "the organization takes pride in my accomplishments at work".

Psychological contract fulfillment has been defined as employees' perception that they received everything their employer promised when they started working, and it has been measured using the psychological contract breach and violation scale developed by Robinson and Morrison (2000). Employees evaluate their psychological contract on a 7-point Likert-type scale, from 1 ("strongly disagree") to 7 ("strongly agree"), with such items as "almost all the promises made by my employer during recruitment have been kept so far", and "so far my employer has done an excellent job of fulfilling its promises to me".

Employer attractiveness has been defined as "the envisioned benefits that a potential employee sees in working for a specific organization" (p. 156) and measured using the employer attractiveness scale developed and validated by Berthon et al. (2005). The scale (EmpAt) includes 25 items covering functional, economic, and psychological benefits that together account for the attractiveness of an employer brand (Alnıaçık & Alnıaçık, 2012). Respondents use a 7-point Likert scale from 1 ("strongly disagree") to 7 ("strongly agree") to indicate their agreement with statements such as "ensures job security within the organization" and "the organization produces innovative products and services".

Our research: a battery of questionnaires

We applied a battery of some of the abovementioned questionnaires to our sample of 26 Croatian organizations: UPZIK by Tkalac Verčič et al. (2009); EmpAt by Berthon et al. (2005), UWES by Schaufeli et al. (2002), psychological contract fulfillment scale by Robinson and Morrison (2000), and POS scale by Eisenberger et al. (1986). We also included a section that measured job satisfaction ("when you think about your job, how satisfied are you?") and ended with a set of sociodemographic questions on gender, age, education, number of years in the organization, and type of job. Data were checked for missing values and assessment of normality. All variables had an approximately normal distribution.

With the assistance of an HR executive in each company, we identified a representative sample of employees across departments, management levels and types of occupation. Managers in each organization circulated emails with an invitation letter that encouraged voluntary participation and contained a link to the online battery of questionnaires. We estimated that respondents should take approximately 25 minutes to complete the questionnaire. The opening page gave a brief explanation of the academic purpose of the study and ensured anonymity and confidentiality.

The final sample in our research consisted of 3,457 employees, 1,805 in the prepandemic group and 1,652 in the pandemic group. The response rate varied from 20% to 45% across organizations. In the entire sample, the gender breakdown was 50% female and 50% male; 4% of the sample were below 25 years old; 27%, 26–35 years; 35%, 36–45 years; 24%, 46–55 years; and the rest, over 50 years old. Just under half the sample (43%) had a secondary school education, while 49% had an undergraduate and graduate degree. Similarly, small proportions had less than a secondary degree (3%) or a postgraduate degree (5%). The sample showed the following distribution of work experience in the current organization: less

Table 5.2 Correlations between employees' attitudes toward their job and internal communication satisfaction (ICS) ($N = 3{,}457$)

Attitude	*Correlation with ICS*	*Interpretation*
Job satisfaction	$r = .636; p = .001$	Job satisfaction correlates significantly with ICS
Employee engagement	$r = .695; p = .001$	Employee engagement correlates significantly with ICS
Employer attractiveness	$r = .897; p = .001$	Employer attraction correlates significantly with ICS
Psychological contract fulfillment	$r = .698; p = .001$	Psychological contract fulfillment correlates significantly with ICS
Perceived organizational support	$r = .748; p = .001$	Perceived organizational support correlates significantly with ICS

than 10 years of experience, 47%; 11–20 years, 29%; 21–30 years, 15%; and more than 30 years, 9%.

Each of the variables on job attitudes showed a significant correlation with internal communication satisfaction (Table 5.2). This supports that idea that organizations cannot manage their employer brand without strategically managing internal communication, since employees' perception of their employer is the most significant element of the organizational brand (Kalinska-Kula & Staniec, 2021). Employees will not be engaged within organizations if they are unhappy with internal communication. Mediating variables such as POS and psychological contract fulfillment were also closely connected to both engagement and internal communication satisfaction, identifying them as additional pieces in the employer branding puzzle. To carefully cultivate all these variables, internal communication must be positioned at the center of the communication process and strategically managed.

Other evaluation methods

Audits can be complex and are defined by the nature, quality, and usefulness of information they generate. These data can be collected through a variety of methods and therefore can take different forms (Dickson, 2009). Interviews and surveys are common – but not the only – approaches to gathering data. Another rather common method, the focus group, is a type of group interview in which opinions are elicited by encouraging interaction among a selected group of employees (Freeman, 2006). The members of this group should share certain characteristics and provide insight into a topic relevant to the audit. Better than any other method, focus groups offer information on which members of the group hold certain opinions and issues, and provide insight into how shared social realities are established (Zorn et al., 2006). Despite the research benefits of focus groups, we were unable to obtain consent from top management of the organizations in our sample to organize such interviews during our research project.

In our project, we also relied on data collection log sheets, a structured form on which specific items need to be filled out. In contrast to a questionnaire that asks about respondents' attitudes, log sheets ask about actual communication practices (Hargie & Tourish, 2009). They are typically filled out immediately after the communication event has occurred by a staff member involved in the event or by an external observer. We used a data collection log sheet to acquire data about the types of channels used in each organization (Table 5.3). We requested that heads of corporate communication and human resources fill out the form together. For each of the channels on the list, we asked them to determine whether they use it and with what frequency (different options were given for each channel). Our objective was to gain deeper insight into connections of specific communication channels with different facets of internal communication satisfaction.

Table 5.3 Data collection log sheet about internal communication channels potentially used in each organization

Digital Channels	
Video posts	Choose an item.
Blogs	Choose an item.
Corporate social network	Choose an item.
If yes, please state which:	Choose an item.
Specially developed internal communication apps	Choose an item.
Group e-mails	Choose an item.
Intranet	Choose an item.
Digital newsletter	Choose an item.
If yes, please state how many times a year:	Choose an item.
Printed Channels	
Printed newsletter	Choose an item.
If yes, please state how many times a year:	Choose an item.
Memos	Choose an item.
Mail sent to home	Choose an item.
Personal Communication	
Meetings of all employees	Choose an item.
Town hall meetings	Choose an item.
Planned, formal discussions with top management	Choose an item.
Educational meetings	Choose an item.
Team building	Choose an item.
Other type(s) of meetings	Choose an item.
If yes, please state which:	Choose an item.
Physical Channels	
Information boards	Choose an item.
Posters	Choose an item.
LCD or other screens	Choose an item.
Other Channels	
If yes, please state which:	Choose an item.

Other methods can be used to evaluate different aspects of internal communication, such as the critical incident technique, the Delphi method, constitutive ethnography, and network analysis (Hargie & Tourish, 2009). Network analysis focuses on relationships between employees instead of their attitudes; these relationships can be exchange relationships or affective relationships. Communication networks can be mapped using sociometry, observation, the small world technique, and archival analysis (de Jong & Zwijze-Koning, 2009). Whatever the objective of an audit, multiple approaches exist to achieve that objective.

Conclusion

Good communication is a prerequisite of organizational success. The goal of this chapter was to present approaches for evaluating internal communication in order to understand and improve it. However, no matter how much or how well internal communication is evaluated, it will be of little benefit unless the organization's leadership is willing to commit resources to improve communication. If executives agree with careful management of communication processes, then evaluation is the obvious first step.

References

Alnıaçık, E., & Alnıaçık, Ü. (2012). Identifying dimensions of attractiveness in employer branding: Effects of age, gender, and current employment status. *Procedia - Social and Behavioral Sciences*, *58*, 1336–1343. https://doi.org/10.1016/j.sbspro.2012.09.1117

Argenti, P. A. (2007). *Strategic corporate communication: A global approach for doing business in the new India*. McGraw-Hill Education.

Bakker, A. B., & Demerouti, E. (2008). Towards a model of work engagement. *Career Development International*, *13*(3), 209–223. https://doi.org/10.1108/13620430810870476

Berthon, P., Ewing, M., & Hah, L. L. (2005). Captivating company: Dimensions of attractiveness in employer branding. *International Journal of Advertising*, *24*(2), 151–172. https://doi.org/10.1080/02650487.2005.11072912

Borovec, K., & Balgač, I. (2017). Contribution of internal communication in predicting job satisfaction among police officers. *Kriminologija & socijalna integracija: časopis za kriminologiju, penologiju i poremećaje u ponašanju*, *25*(1), 17–33. https://doi.org/10.31299/ksi.25.1.1

Broom, G. M., & Dozier, D. M. (1990). *Using research in public relations: Applications to program management*. Prentice Hall.

Clampitt, P. G., & Downs, C. W. (1993). Employee perceptions of the relationship between communication and productivity: A field study. *The Journal of Business Communication (1973)*, *30*(1), 5–28. https://doi.org/10.1177/002194369303000101

de Jong, M. D., & Zwijze-Koning, K. H. (2009). Communication network analysis. In O. Hargie, & D. Tourish (Eds.), *Auditing organizational communication: A handbook of research, theory and practice* (pp. 169–186). Routledge.

DeWine, S. (1994). International communication association audit. In R. Rubin, P. Palmgreen, & H. Sypher (Eds.), *Communication research measures: A sourcebook* (pp. 193–205). The Guilford Press.

Dickson, D. (2009). The focus group approach. In O. Hargie, & D. Tourish (Eds.), *Auditing organizational communication: A handbook of research, theory and practice* (pp. 123–142). Routledge.

Dickson, D., Reiney, S., & Hargie, O. (2003). Communication sensitive business issues: Part 1. *Corporate Communications*, *8*(1), 35–43. https://doi.org/10.1108/13563280310458902

Downs, C. (1988). *Communication audits*. Scott Foresman & Company.

Downs, C. W., & Adrian, A. (2004). *Assessing organizational communication: Strategic communication audits*. The Guilford Press.

Downs, C. W., & Hazen, M. D. (1977). A factor analytic study of communication satisfaction. *The Journal of Business Communication*, *14*(3), 63–74. https://doi.org/10.1177/002194367701400306

Downs, C., DeWine, S., & Greenbaum, H. (1994). Measures of organizational communication. In R. Rubin, P. Palmgreen, & H. Sypher (Eds.), *Communication research measures: A sourcebook* (pp. 57–78). The Guilford Press.

Downs, C. W. (1994). Communication satisfaction questionnaire. In R. Rubin, P. Palmgreen, & H. Sypher (Eds.), *Communication research measures: A sourcebook* (pp. 114–119). The Guilford Press.

Eisenberger, R., Huntington, R., Hutchison, S., & Sowa, D. (1986). Perceived organizational support. *Journal of Applied Psychology*, *71*(3), 500–507. https://doi.org/10.1037/0021-9010.71.3.500

Forman, J., & Argenti, P. A. (2005). How corporate communication influences strategy implementation, reputation and the corporate brand: An exploratory qualitative study. *Corporate Reputation Review*, *8*(3), 245–264. https://doi.org/10.1057/palgrave.crr.1540253

Freeman, T. (2006). 'Best practice' in focus group research: Making sense of different views. *Journal of Advanced Nursing*, *56*(5), 491–497. https://doi.org/10.1111/j.1365-2648.2006.04043.x

Goldhaber, G. M. (2002). Communication audits in the age of the internet. *Management Communication Quarterly*, *15*(3), 451–457. https://doi.org/10.1177/0893318902153007

Gray, J., & Laidlaw, H. (2004). Improving the measurement of communications satisfaction. *Management Communication Quarterly*, *17*(3), 425–448. https://doi.org/10.1177/0893318903257980

Greenbaum, H. H., Clampitt, P., & Willihnganz, S. (1988). Organizational communication: An examination of four instruments. *Management Communication Quarterly*, *2*(2), 245–282. https://doi.org/10.1177/0893318988002002008

Grunig, J. E., & Hunt, T. (1984). *Managing public relations*. Holt, Rinehart and Winston.

Hallberg, U. E., & Schaufeli, W. B. (2006). "Same same" but different? Can work engagement be discriminated from job involvement and organizational commitment? *European Psychologist*, *11*(2), 119–127. https://doi.org/10.1027/1016-9040.11.2.119

Hargie, O., & Tourish, D. (Eds.) (2000). *Handbook of communication audits for organizations*. Routledge.

Hargie, O., & Tourish, D. (Eds.) (2009). *Auditing organizational communication: A handbook of research, theory and practice*. Routledge.

Jiang, H., & Men, R. L. (2017). Creating an engaged workforce: The impact of authentic leadership, transparent organizational communication, and work-life enrichment. *Communication Research*, *44*(2), 225–243. https://doi.org/10.1177/0093650215613137

Kopec, J. A. (1982). The communication audit. *Public Relations Journal*, *39*, 24–27.

Kalinska-Kula, M., & Staniec, I. (2021). Employer branding and organizational attractiveness: Current employees' perspective. *European Research Studies Journal, XXIV*, *1*, 583–603. https://doi.org/10.35808/ersj/1982

Lalić, D., Marjanović, U., & Lalić, B. (2012). The influence of social networks on communication satisfaction within the organizations. In M. Cruz-Cunha, P. Goncalves, N. Lopes, E. Miranda, & G. Putnik (Eds.), *Handbook of research on business social networking: Organizational, managerial, and technological dimensions* (pp. 545–566). IGI Global.

Lindenmann, W. K. (1993). An 'Effectiveness Yardstick' to measure public relations success. *Public Relations Quarterly*, *38*(1), 7–9.

Men, L. R. (2014a). Why leadership matters to internal communication: Linking transformational leadership, symmetrical communication, and employee outcomes. *Journal of Public Relations Research*, *26*(3), 256–279. https://doi.org/10.1080/1062726X.2014.908719

Men, L. R. (2014b). Internal reputation management: The impact of authentic leadership and transparent communication. *Corporate Reputation Review*, *17*(4), 254–272. https://doi.org/10.1057/crr.2014.14

Men, L. R., & Yue, C. A. (2019). Creating a positive emotional culture: Effect of internal communication and impact on employee supportive behaviors. *Public Relations Review*, *45*(3), 101764. https://doi.org/10.1016/j.pubrev.2019.03.001

Men, L. R., Yue, C. A., & Liu, Y. (2020). "Vision, passion, and care:" The impact of charismatic executive leadership communication on employee trust and support for organizational change. *Public Relations Review*, *46*(3), 101927. https://doi.org/10.1016/j.pubrev.2020.101927

Men, R. L., & Bowen, S. A. (2017). *Excellence in internal communication management*. Business Expert Press.

Millar, R., & Tracey, A. (2009). The interview approach. In O. Hargie, & D. Tourish (Eds.), *Auditing organizational communication: A handbook of research, theory and practice* (pp. 98–122). Routledge.

Pološki Vokić, N., Rimac Bilušić, M., & Najjar, D. (2020). Building organizational trust through internal communication. *Corporate Communications: An International Journal*, *26*(1), 70–83. https://doi.org/10.1108/CCIJ-01-2020-0023

Quinn, D., & Hargie, O. (2004). Internal communication audits: A case study. *Corporate Communications: An International Journal*, *9*(2), 146–158. https://doi.org/10.1108/13563280410534348

Roberts, K. H., & O'Reilly, C. A. (1974). Measuring organizational communication. *Journal of Applied Psychology*, *59*(3), 321–326. https://doi.org/10.1037/h0036660

Robinson, S. L., & Morrison, E. W. (2000). The development of psychological contract breach and violation: A longitudinal study. *Journal of Organizational Behavior*, *21*(5), 525–546. https://doi.org/10.1002/1099-1379(200008)21:5<525::AID-JOB40>3.0.CO;2-T

Robson, P. J., & Tourish, D. (2005). Managing internal communication: An organizational case study. *Corporate Communications: An International Journal*, *10*(3), 213–222. https://doi.org/10.1108/13563280510614474

Schaufeli, W. B., & Bakker, A. B. (2004). Job demands, job resources, and their relationship with burnout and engagement: A multi-sample study. *Journal of Organizational Behavior*, *25*(3), 293–315. https://doi.org/10.1002/job.248

Schaufeli, W. B., Martínez, I. M., Marques Pinto, A., Salanova, M., & Bakker, A. B. (2002). Burnout and engagement in university students. *Journal of Cross-Cultural Psychology*, *33*(5), 464–481. https://doi.org/10.1177/0022022102033005003

Seidman, I. E. (1998). *Interviewing as qualitative research: A guide for researchers in education and the social sciences* (2nd ed.). Teachers College Press.

Sinčić Ćorić, D., Pološki Vokić, N., & Tkalac Verčič, A. (2020). Does good internal communication enhance life satisfaction? *Journal of Communication Management*, *24*(4), 363–376. https://doi.org/10.1108/JCOM-11-2019-0146

Stone, B. C. (1995). Strategic marketing and communications audits. *Journal of Health Care Marketing*, *15*(4), 54–57.

Tkalac Verčič, A. (2021). The impact of employee engagement, organisational support and employer branding on internal communication satisfaction. *Public Relations Review*, *47*(1), 102009. https://doi.org/10.1016/j.pubrev.2021.102009

Tkalac Verčič, A., & Pološki Vokić, N. (2017). Engaging employees through internal communication. *Public Relations Review*, *43*(5), 885–893. https://doi.org/10.1016/j.pubrev.2017.04.005

Tkalac Verčič, A., & Špoljarić, A. (2020). Managing internal communication: How the choice of channels affects internal communication satisfaction. *Public Relations Review*, *46*(3), 101926. https://doi.org/10.1016/j.pubrev.2020.101926

Tkalac Verčič, A., Pološki Vokić, N., & Sinčić Ćorić, D. (2009). Razvoj mjernog instrumenta za procjenu zadovoljstva internom komunikacijom [Development of the internal communication satisfaction questionnaire]. *Društvena istraživanja: časopis za opća društvena pitanja*, *18*(1–2), 175–202.

Tourish, D., & Hargie, O. (2009). *Auditing organizational communication: A handbook of research, theory and practice*. Routledge.

Varona, F. (1996). Relationship between communication satisfaction and organizational commitment three Guatemalan organizations. *The Journal of Business Communication*, *33*(2), 111–140. https://doi.org/10.1177/002194369603300203

Yamaguchi, I. (2017). Instruments for organizational communication assessment for Japanese care Facilities. *Corporate Communications: An International Journal*, *22*(4), 471–485. https://doi.org/10.1108/CCIJ-04-2017-0045

Zorn, T. E., Roper, J., Broadfoot, K., & Kay Weaver, C. (2006). Focus groups as sites of influential interaction: Building communicative self-efficacy and effecting attitudinal change in discussing controversial topics. *Journal of Applied Communication Research*, *34*(2), 115–140. https://doi.org/10.1080/00909880600573965

6 Internal communication satisfaction

The research project from which this book emerged aimed to model internal communication and its processes, and one of the major variables in the model was internal communication satisfaction (ICS). We wanted to explore what factors affect it, what factors it affects, and how it relates to workplace attitudes. In this chapter we explain why we focused on communication satisfaction in our research, and we argue that evaluating and managing communication satisfaction can have a substantial impact on organizational performance.

Putting satisfaction in context

Communication satisfaction is based on the general concept of satisfaction, which is a common theme in studies of human behavior. Satisfaction is a sign of psychological health and well-being. Satisfying communication indicates psychological adjustment, while unsatisfying communication can be a symptom of pathological states (Hecht, 1978a). Our ability to communicate well with others is important for establishing satisfying relationships (Rossiter & Pearce, 1975). Satisfaction is an important variable in various theoretical perspectives, including exchange theory, behaviorism, cognitivism, and hedonism, though these approaches may not agree on what causes satisfaction or on how it influences the behavior of individuals or organizations (Hecht, 1978a).

Communication satisfaction is an important outcome when evaluating the communication behavior of individuals, groups, and organizations. By measuring such satisfaction, organizations can create a framework for evaluating their communication processes (Hecht, 1978a) and thereby optimize their communication strategies. Assessment of communication satisfaction can aid the evaluation of internal communication in three ways (Hecht, 1978a). It can be used to analyze the many factors potentially involved in such communication, such as engagement and organizational support; it can be used to clarify how the influence of those factors depends on type of communication, such as communication with superiors or feedback; and it can drive the improvement of communication

DOI: 10.4324/9781003200109-6

skills. Other conceptualizations define communication satisfaction in terms of the fulfillment of psychological traits, but Hecht (1978a) defines satisfaction as "environmental reinforcement of the individual's discrimination of stimuli" (p. 62), stipulating associations between personal internal state and environmental factors.

Studying ICS is important for the same reasons that Spector (1997) emphasized when studying job satisfaction. Communication satisfaction can reflect to what extent employees feel respected and fairly treated, and to what extent the organization functions smoothly. Indeed, greater communication satisfaction can improve organizational function. Diagnosing areas of communication dissatisfaction can identify "problem areas".

Communication satisfaction within organizations

A prominent view holds that an organization's performance suffers when communication is poor; good communication, conversely, means better performance and overall effectiveness (Roberts & O'Reilly, 1973). This view is partially based on Likert and Hayes' work (1957) in which they approached communication as a variable that mediates the influence of leadership behavior and organizational structure on job satisfaction, productivity, and profits.

In the early 1970s, the organizational division of the International Communication Association conducted research on communication in organizations (Jeffres, 2008) which led the Association to classify studies on internal communication into three major categories (Goldhaber, 1993): first, studies of information flow within organizations; second, studies of the content of received messages; and third, studies of attitudes, feelings, and perceptions of communicators about the communication system and its parts. Subsequent research confirmed the usefulness of this audit for increasing positive organizational outcomes (Hargie et al., 2002).

This audit in the early 1970s examined employees' satisfaction with communication within their organizations. Downs and Hazen (1977) operationalized the construct of communication satisfaction and developed a corresponding instrument in order to explore the relationship between job satisfaction and communication, with the ultimate goal of developing a theory of communication in organizations (Clampitt & Girard, 1993). Their construct went on to become a successful stream of research on organizational communication (Varona, 1996). This research has supported the idea that communication satisfaction is strongly connected to job satisfaction, such that the more satisfied employees are with communication, the more they are satisfied with their jobs (Hargie & Tourish, 2009) and the more likely they are to remain with the organization (Downs & Adrian, 2004).

Despite these early successes measuring communication satisfaction, we agree with Ruck and Welch (2012) that "minimal attention has been given to what employees would like their organizations to communicate" (p. 295), and with Chen et al. (2006) that "member satisfaction with organisational communication practices has been ignored" (p. 242). We believe that communication satisfaction is a key variable in managing internal communication processes, so we placed it at the center of our modeling in the research project from which this book emerged. For the same reason, we prefer to refer to such satisfaction as ICS.

Defining ICS

In describing communication satisfaction, Hecht (1978a) defined it as a socioemotional outcome of communication interactions, while Downs and Hazen (1977) saw it as the sum of an individual's satisfaction with relationship and information flow variables. More recently, ICS has been described as an individual's satisfaction with various aspects of communication in interpersonal, group and organizational contexts (Tsai et al., 2009). Carrière et al. (2007) consider it a consequence of formal and informal communication activities. These activities share the goal of disseminating information by members of the organization, and they may transfer information horizontally, downward, or upward. We prefer the perhaps simpler definition of ICS as satisfaction with different aspects of communication within organizations (Crino & White, 1981). It is important to emphasize, however, that ICS is related, but not identical to, communication practices: the practices are the antecedent, while ICS is the consequent (Carrière & Bourque, 2009).

We operationalize ICS as an attitudinal variable: it measures how much employees like or dislike internal communication in their organizations. Occasionally, we consider these attitudes in the aggregate as a single global attitude, such as when we wish to focus on the effects of that attitude. Most of the time, however, we treat ICS as a collection of attitudes about various aspects of communication in the organization. Our goal is to explore which elements of communication influence levels of satisfaction. It seems that the combination of global and dimensional approaches gives the most complete picture of ICS in organizations.

Dimensions of ICS

Although some work suggests that there exists a general concept of communication satisfaction (Varona, 1996), more evidence supports a multidimensional concept (Clampitt & Downs, 1993; Crino & White, 1981; Gray & Laidlaw, 2004; Tkalac Verčič et al., 2009), although researchers differ in the number of dimensions. The exact dimensionality of ICS remains an open question, yet it is clear that measuring it only in a global sense fails to support precise assessments of satisfaction or provide detailed insights into specific aspects of communication environment.

A multidimensional approach, in contrast, can clarify factors that influence, and are influenced by, dimensions of ICS. Thus, we adopted this approach in our research project in order to measure the effects of different ICS dimensions on employee engagement and employer brand.

Most multidimensional conceptualizations of ICS include communication climate, amount of information that employees receive, and receptivity of management toward upward communication (Downs & Hazen, 1977; Hargie et al., 2002; Mohr & Sohi, 1995). Hecht (1978b) proposed three dimensions, but these explained only half the variance in their study, while Putti et al. (1990) recognized a relational dimension, defined as satisfaction with relationships; and an informational dimension, defined as satisfaction with information content and flow. Similarly, Pincus (1986) specified three dimensions – relational, informational and general – and concluded that the dimensions overlapped to some extent, leading him to propose a second-order factor structure. Decades later, Gray and Laidlaw (2004) identified a second-order factor structure based on informational and relational dimensions.

The dimensional complexity of ICS highlights the need for standardized questionnaires with good psychometric qualities. The most cited instrument for measuring ICS is the Communication Satisfaction Questionnaire developed by Downs and Hazen (1977) nearly 50 years ago. The fact that this questionnaire was developed so long ago and in a US context, which is the same country that has produced most instruments for assessing ICS (Yamaguchi, 2017), prompted us to construct an instrument potentially more appropriate for international use. We originally developed this new scale, which we named the Internal Communication Satisfaction Questionnaire (ICSQ), in Croatian (Tkalac Verčič et al., 2009) with eight dimensions and 32 items. We describe the Croatian ICSQ in more detail in Chapter 5. The Croatian ICSQ proved to be reliable and valid in numerous studies (Borovec & Balgač, 2017; Lalić et al., 2012; Pološki Vokić et al., 2020; Sinčić Ćorić et al., 2020; Tkalac Verčič & Pološki Vokić, 2017; Tkalac Verčič & Špoljarić, 2020), so we designed and validated an English version intended for employees who speak English as a second language and use it routinely within their organizations (Tkalac Verčič et al., 2021). This version also proved reliable, and confirmatory factor analysis revealed good internal consistency for all dimensions.

The Croatian and English versions of the ICSQ explore the following eight dimensions of ICS (Table 6.1): (1) *satisfaction with feedback* (SwF), which measures satisfaction with information about how well an employee is performing, and about the consequences and contribution of his/her work for the organization's success; (2) *satisfaction with communication with one's immediate superior* (SwIS), which evaluates formal and informal communication with the immediate superior, and measures how much the superior pays attention to, and listens to, the employee; (3) *satisfaction with horizontal communication* (SwHC), which measures

Table 6.1 Dimensions and items on the internal communication satisfaction questionnaire (ICSQ)

Satisfaction with Feedback	
1.	Information on the consequences of doing my job poorly
2.	Information on how much I contribute to the organization's success
3.	Information on how much my job is appreciated within the organization
4.	Feedback on how well I do my job
Satisfaction with Communication with Immediate Superior	
5.	Availability of my immediate superior
6.	How well my immediate superior is informed about the problems that I may encounter at work
7.	How well my immediate superior understands my problems
8.	Recognition of my potential by my immediate superior
Satisfaction with Horizontal Communication	
9.	Availability of colleagues
10.	How successfully I am able to communicate with the members of my team
11.	The outcomes of communicating with colleagues
12.	Readiness of my colleagues to accept critical feedback
Satisfaction with Informal Communication	
13.	The number of decisions made based on informal communications
14.	The amount of gossip in the organization
15.	The amount of time I spend in informal communication
16.	Usefulness of information transferred through informal channels
Satisfaction with Information about the Organization	
17.	Information on work protocols
18.	Information on revenues, profit and the financial status of the organization
19.	Information on changes in the organization
20.	Information on legal regulations that affect the organization's operations
Satisfaction with Communication Climate	
21.	How much communication within the organization helps me feel I am an important part of the organization
22.	How much communication within the organization helps me to identify with the organization
23.	How much communication within the organization promotes organizational values
24.	How much communication within the organization encourages me to accomplish the organization's goals
Satisfaction with the Quality of Communication Media	
25.	Communication media (e.g., written announcements, intranet, oral communication)
26.	The possibility of communicating through new media
27.	Quality of communication through new media
28.	The mode of communication that others choose to communicate with me
Satisfaction with Communication in Meetings	
29.	How well organized are the meetings that I participate in
30.	Usefulness of information received in meetings
31.	Receiving information relevant for job accomplishment on time
32.	Duration of meetings

availability of colleagues for communication, ease of communication with them, and their readiness to accept criticism; (4) *satisfaction with informal communication* (SwIC), which measures satisfaction with the frequency of informal gatherings, the number of decisions based on informal communication, the amount of gossip in the organization, and the usefulness and accuracy of informal information; (5) *satisfaction with information about the organization* (SwIO), which measures satisfaction with information about processes important for the organization's functioning and success, such as finances and legal issues affecting organizational operations and work procedures; (6) *satisfaction with communication climate* (SwCC), which measures satisfaction with information that promotes organizational values and goals, such as measuring how much communication helps employees feel important for the organization and identify with it; (7) *satisfaction with the quality of communication media* (SwQM), which measures satisfaction with different media, their accessibility and their ease of use; and (8) *satisfaction with communication in meetings* (SwCM), which measures satisfaction with the organization and length of meetings, as well as the usefulness of information shared during them.

Since 2009, we and others have applied this instrument in various organizational contexts. For example, we used it to explore the relationship between ICS and employee engagement, employer attractiveness, and perceived organizational support (Tkalac Verčič, 2021). We observed a significant positive relationship between ICS and all the other variables. We also used it to explore employee preferences for internal communication channels (Tkalac Verčič & Špoljarić, 2020). We found that ICS was higher among employees who used rich media, while lean media gave mixed results. We used the questionnaire to explore the relationship between ICS and life satisfaction, and we found that all eight dimensions of ICS correlated significantly with life satisfaction (Sinčić Ćorić et al., 2020); the correlations were strongest in the case of satisfaction with informal communication and with communication climate. In other work, we found that three ICS dimensions were more relevant to employee engagement: satisfaction with feedback, informal communication, and communication during meetings (Tkalac Verčič & Pološki Vokić, 2017). In fact, we later found that six of the eight ICS dimensions and three dimensions of employee engagement were significant predictors of employer attractiveness (Špoljarić & Tkalac Verčič, 2022).

ICS in our research project

During the research project from which this book emerged, we collected ICS data from 3,457 employees in Croatia-based organizations with 60–9,000 employees that were judged to be "typical" organizations (see Chapter 5).

Data were collected from 1,805 employees before the COVID-19 pandemic and from 1,652 employees during the pandemic.

We wanted to see which ICS dimensions were associated with higher satisfaction, as well as how satisfaction changed after organizations switched to a home office model when countries began locking down during the pandemic. The ICS dimension with which respondents were most satisfied was satisfaction with horizontal communication, reflecting that employees are often most satisfied with communication with their colleagues and other members of their work teams (e.g., Sinčić Ćorić et al., 2020). It seems that no matter the circumstances, employees always find a way to communicate with their peers. Employees in our study were least satisfied with feedback, and this ICS dimension has similarly proven to be more problematic than other dimensions in our previous work (e.g., Tkalac Verčič & Pološki Vokić, 2017). Apparently employees often feel that they could receive more information about how much they contribute to the organization, how well they perform their job and how much their organization appreciates them.

As shown in Figure 6.1, during the pandemic, all eight dimensions of ICS significantly increased, with satisfaction with feedback showing the second largest increase. Organizations provided more feedback to employees, presumably because of remote working, and the communication climate changed substantially. The need to "pull together" in the face of shared problems and uncertainties united employees and helped them identify with the organization. These changes demonstrate that small management efforts and investments in internal communication

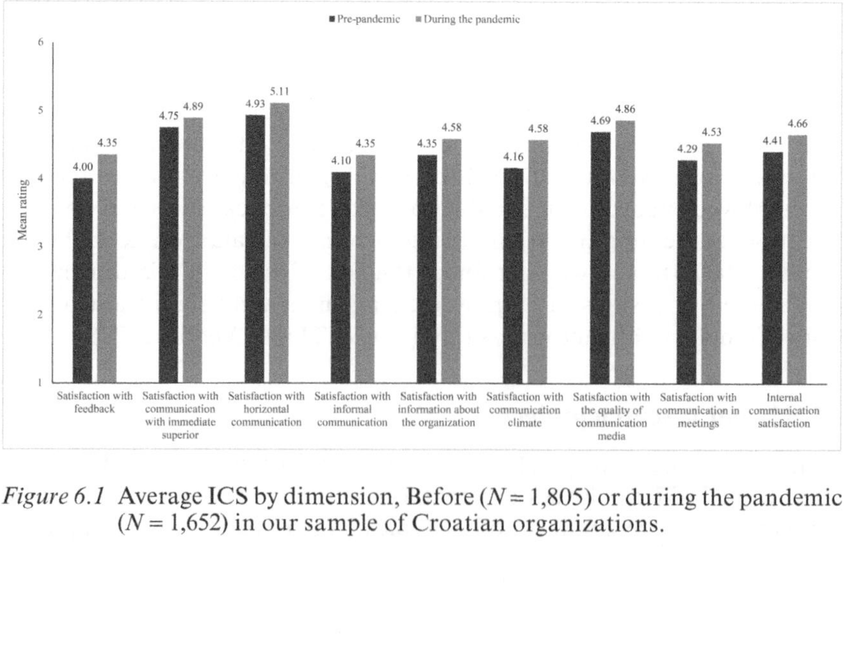

Figure 6.1 Average ICS by dimension, Before ($N = 1{,}805$) or during the pandemic ($N = 1{,}652$) in our sample of Croatian organizations.

can produce significant results. The increase in ICS during the pandemic is even more notable given that neither job satisfaction nor engagement changed over the same period, even though both variables are connected to ICS and often considered to overlap with it.

We identified several interesting trends when we examined how ICS distributed across different demographic subgroups among the respondents (Table 6.2). Women were more satisfied than men overall and on all dimensions except satisfaction with communication with immediate superior and satisfaction with horizontal communication, which did not differ significantly between the genders. ICS increased with level of education and management rank, perhaps reflecting the fact that such (more educated or more highly ranked) employees determine the way communication is managed. Conversely, satisfaction overall and on all eight dimensions decreased with age. Employees who are male or older seem to expect more from their employers, especially when it comes to information about them. Mirroring the age trend, employees become less satisfied the longer they work for an organization.

Benefits of higher ICS

In previous work with different samples of organizations, we found evidence that ICS, particularly satisfaction with feedback, informal communication, and communication during meetings, is an antecedent of employee engagement (Tkalac Verčič & Pološki Vokić, 2017), which concurs with studies in other countries (Abraham, 2012; Karanges et al., 2015; Ruck & Welch, 2012). We also discovered that all eight ICS dimensions, particularly satisfaction with informal communication and satisfaction with communication climate, correlated significantly with life satisfaction (Sinčić Ćorić et al., 2020). In more recent work (Tkalac Verčič et al., 2021), we found further evidence that ICS is related to employee engagement, and that psychological contract agreement and perceived organizational support mediate this relationship. Although that study examined ICS globally rather than by dimensions, the results highlight the need for organizations to understand all elements of internal communication in order to have a good grasp of employee communication behavior and attitudes.

Although our research project cannot necessarily clarify what causes ICS or how it influences the behavior of individuals or organizations, our data do identify clear connections between ICS and certain organizational variables. In particular, we focused on potential relationships of satisfaction with employee perceptions of internal communication and work attitudes. This focus reflects the well-established relationship between work attitudes and meaningful work outcomes, at the individual and organizational levels (Carrière et al., 2007). Analyzing our sample of Croatian employers, we discovered that overall ICS significantly and

Table 6.2 Average ICS by dimension for different demographic subgroups in our sample of Croatian organizations

Stratifying Variable	*Classes of Variable*	*ICS Dimension*								
		SwF	*SwIS*	*SwHC*	*SwIC*	*SwIO*	*SwCC*	*SwQM*	*SwCM*	*ICS*
Gender	Male	4.1	4.8	5.0	4.2	4.3	4.3	4.7	4.3	4.5
	Female	4.3	4.8	5.0	4.3	4.7	4.4	4.9	4.5	4.6
Age	18–25	4.7	5.3	5.4	4.7	4.9	4.9	5.2	4.8	5.0
	26–35	4.4	5.0	5.3	4.5	4.7	4.7	5.1	4.6	4.8
	36–45	4.2	4.9	5.1	4.3	4.5	4.4	4.8	4.4	4.6
	46–55	4.0	4.7	4.9	4.1	4.3	4.2	4.6	4.3	4.4
	>55	3.9	4.7	4.8	4.0	4.1	4.2	4.5	4.2	4.3
Length of service	≤10	4.4	5.0	5.2	4.4	4.8	4.6	5.0	4.6	4.8
	11–20	4.1	4.8	5.0	4.2	4.5	4.3	4.8	4.4	4.5
	21–30	3.7	4.5	4.7	3.9	4.0	4.0	4.4	4.0	4.2
	>30	3.8	4.6	4.7	3.8	3.9	3.9	4.2	4.1	4.1
Level of education	Primary	3.5	4.2	4.6	3.4	3.4	3.6	3.5	3.7	3.7
	Secondary	4.1	4.7	4.9	4.1	4.3	4.3	4.5	4.3	4.4
	Undergraduate	4.0	4.7	5.0	4.2	4.3	4.3	4.8	4.4	4.5
	Graduate	4.2	4.9	5.1	4.3	4.7	4.4	5.0	4.5	4.6
	Doctoral	4.4	5.0	5.1	4.4	4.8	4.4	5.1	4.6	4.7
Management level	Not a part of	4.3	4.9	5.1	4.3	4.5	4.6	4.9	4.5	4.7
	Lower	4.5	5.0	5.1	4.4	4.8	4.7	5.1	4.6	4.8
	Middle	4.8	5.3	5.3	4.6	5.0	5.0	5.3	4.8	5.0
	Upper	5.3	5.7	5.5	4.9	5.5	5.4	5.7	5.1	5.4

Legend: SwCC, satisfaction with communication climate; SwCM, satisfaction with communication in meetings; SwF, satisfaction with feedback; SwHC, satisfaction with horizontal communication; SwIC, satisfaction with informal communication; SwIO, satisfaction with information about the organization; SwIS, satisfaction with communication with immediate superior; SwQM, satisfaction with the quality of communication media.

positively correlated with overall employer attractiveness (Pološki Vokić et al., 2021). Seven of eight ICS dimensions were connected to all five attractiveness dimensions. The most significant dimensions for attractiveness proved to be "satisfaction with feedback" and "satisfaction with communication climate". These results again emphasize the importance, when analyzing ICS, of understanding how the organizational context creates connections between internal communication processes and employees' perceptions of their employers. They also show the importance of cultivating informal dimensions of internal communication for creating a positive communication environment.

Conclusion

ICS measures how people feel about internal communication in their organizations. Such satisfaction can – all other things being equal – explain differences in organizational performance. Increasing ICS through proper auditing and management of internal communication can improve productivity, quality of services and products, and levels of innovation, while reducing absenteeism, strikes, and costs (Clampitt & Downs, 1993).

ICS can be assessed globally as general satisfaction with internal communication, or it can be analyzed according to one of several dimensions. In this chapter we demonstrate application of the ICSQ, a questionnaire that conceptualizes ICS along eight empirically supported dimensions. We show how applying the ICSQ to a large sample of Croatian organizations allowed us to detect that even without a substantial increase in investment in internal communication, organizations were able to weather the shift to lockdown and home office caused by the COVID-19 pandemic. The pandemic forced organizations to pay more attention to internal communication, and some dimensions of ICS increased significantly as a result. As our work shows, it pays to pay attention.

References

Abraham, S. (2012). Job satisfaction as an antecedent to employee engagement. *SIES Journal of Management*, *8*(2), 27–36.

Borovec, K., & Balgač, I. (2017). Contribution of internal communication in predicting job satisfaction among police officers. *Kriminologija & socijalna integracija: časopis za kriminologiju, penologiju i poremećaje u ponašanju*, *25*(1), 17–33. https://doi.org/10.31299/ksi.25.1.1

Carrière, J., & Bourque, C. (2009). The effects of organizational communication on job satisfaction and organizational commitment in a land ambulance service and the mediating role of communication satisfaction. *Career Development International*, *14*(1), 29–49. https://doi.org/10.1108/13620430910933565

Carrière, J., Bourque, C., & Bonaccio, S. (2007). The role of communication satisfaction as a mediator between an organizations internal communication systems and two job outcomes: Job satisfaction and organizational commitment. *Proceedings of the Marketing Division of Administrative Sciences Association of Canada (ASAC) Annual Conference* (pp. 60–75). ASAC.

Chen, J. C., Silverthorne, C., & Hung, J. Y. (2006). Organization communication, job stress, organizational commitment, and job performance of accounting professionals in Taiwan and America. *Leadership & Organization Development Journal*, *27*(4), 242–249. https://doi.org/10.1108/01437730610666000

Clampitt, P. G., & Downs, C. W. (1993). Employee perceptions of the relationship between communication and productivity: A field study. *The Journal of Business Communication (1973)*, *30*(1), 5–28. https://doi.org/10.1177/002194369303000101

Clampitt, P. G., & Girard, D. (1993). Communication satisfaction: A useful construct? *Atlantic Journal of Communication*, *1*(2), 84–102. https://doi.org/10.1080/15456879309367255

Crino, M. D., & White, M. C. (1981). Satisfaction in communication: An examination of the Downs-Hazen measure. *Psychological Reports*, *49*(3), 831–838. https://doi.org/10.2466/pr0.1981.49.3.831

Downs, C. W., & Adrian, A. D. (Eds.). (2004). *Assessing organizational communication: Strategic communication audits*. Guilford Press.

Downs, C. W., & Hazen, M. D. (1977). A factor analytic study of communication satisfaction. *The Journal of Business Communication (1973)*, *14*(3), 63–73. https://doi.org/10.1177/002194367701400306

Goldhaber, G. M. (1993). *Organizational communication* (6th ed.). Brown & Benchmark.

Gray, J., & Laidlaw, H. (2004). Improving the measurement of communication satisfaction. *Management Communication Quarterly*, *17*(3), 425–448. https://doi.org/10.1177/0893318903257980

Hargie, O. E., & Tourish, D. E. (2009). *Auditing organizational communication: A handbook of research, theory and practice*. Routledge.

Hargie, O., Tourish, D., & Wilson, N. (2002). Communication audits and the effects of increased information: A follow-up study. *The Journal of Business Communication (1973)*, *39*(4), 414–436. https://doi.org/10.1177/002194360203900402

Hecht, M. L. (1978a). The conceptualization and measurement of interpersonal communication satisfaction. *Human Communication Research*, *4*(3), 253–264. https://doi.org/10.1111/j.1468-2958.1978.tb00614.x

Hecht, M. L. (1978b). The conceptualization and measurement of interpersonal communication satisfaction. *Human Communication Research*, *4*(3), 253–264. https://doi.org/10.1111/j.1468-2958.1978.tb00614.x

Jeffres, L. W. (2008). An Urban Communication Audit: Measuring aspects of a 'Communicative City'. *International Communication Gazette*, *70*(3–4), 257–273. https://doi.org/10.1177/1748048508089951

Karanges, E., Johnston, K., Beatson, A., & Lings, I. (2015). The influence of internal communication on employee engagement: A pilot study. *Public Relations Review*, *41*(1), 129–131. https://doi.org/10.1016/j.pubrev.2014.12.003

Lalić, D., Marjanović, U., & Lalić, B. (2012). The influence of social networks on communication satisfaction within the organizations. In M. Cruz-Cunha, P. Goncalves, N. Lopes, E. Miranda, & G. Putnik (Eds.), *Handbook of research on business social networking: Organizational, managerial, and technological dimensions* (pp. 545–566). IGI Global.

Likert, R., & Hayes, S. P. (Eds.). (1957). *Some applications of behavioural research*. UNESCO.

Mohr, J. J., & Sohi, R. S. (1995). Communication flows in distribution channels: Impact on assessments of communication quality and satisfaction. *Journal of Retailing*, *71*(4), 393–415. https://doi.org/10.1016/0022-4359(95)90020-9

Pincus, J. D. (1986). Communication satisfaction, job satisfaction, and job performance. *Human Communication Research*, *12*(3), 395–419. https://doi.org/10.1111/j.1468-2958.1986.tb00084.x

Pološki Vokić, N., Rimac Bilušić, M., & Najjar, D. (2020). Building organizational trust through internal communication. *Corporate Communications: An International Journal*, *26*(1), 70–83. https://doi.org/10.1108/CCIJ-01-2020-0023

Pološki Vokić, N., Tkalac Verčič, A., & Sinčić Ćorić, D. (2021). *Strategic internal communication for effective internal employer branding* [Unpublished manuscript]. Faculty of Economics and Business Zagreb, University of Zagreb.

Putti, J. M., Aryee, S., & Phua, J. (1990). Communication relationship satisfaction and organizational commitment. *Group & Organization Studies*, *15*(1), 44–52. https://doi.org/10.1177/105960119001500104

Roberts, K. H., & O'Reilly III, C. A. (1973). *Some problems in measuring organizational communication*. Institute of Industrial Relations, University of California.

Rossiter, C. M., & Pearce, W. B. (1975). *Communicating personally*. Bobbs-Merrill.

Ruck, K., & Welch, M. (2012). Valuing internal communication; management and employee perspectives. *Public Relations Review*, *38*(2), 294–302. https://doi.org/10.1016/j.pubrev.2011.12.016

Sinčić Ćorić, D., Pološki Vokić, N., & Tkalac Verčič, A. (2020). Does good internal communication enhance life satisfaction? *Journal of Communication Management*, *24*(4), 363–376. https://doi.org/10.1108/JCOM-11-2019-0146

Spector, P. E. (1997). *Job satisfaction: Application, assessment, causes, and consequences* (Vol. 3). Sage Publications.

Špoljarić, A., & Tkalac Verčič, A. (2022). Internal communication satisfaction and employee engagement as determinants of the employer brand. *Journal of Communication Management*, *26*(1), 130–148. https://doi.org/10.1108/JCOM-01-2021-0011

Tkalac Verčič, A. (2021). The impact of employee engagement, organisational support and employer branding on internal communication satisfaction. *Public Relations Review*, *47*(1), 102009. https://doi.org/10.1016/j.pubrev.2021.102009

Tkalac Verčič, A., & Pološki Vokić, N. (2017). Engaging employees through internal communication. *Public Relations Review*, *43*(5), 885–893. https://doi.org/10.1016/j.pubrev.2017.04.005

Tkalac Verčič, A., & Špoljarić, A. (2020). Managing internal communication: How the choice of channels affects internal communication satisfaction. *Public Relations Review*, *46*(3), 101926. https://doi.org/10.1016/j.pubrev.2020.101926

Tkalac Verčič, A., Pološki Vokić, N., & Sinčić Ćorić, D. (2009). Razvoj mjernog instrumenta za procjenu zadovoljstva internom komunikacijom [Development of the internal communication satisfaction questionnaire]. *Društvena istraživanja: časopis za opća društvena pitanja*, *18*(1–2), 175–202.

Tkalac Verčič, A., Sinčić Ćorić, D., & Pološki Vokić, N. (2021). Measuring internal communication satisfaction: Validating the internal communication satisfaction questionnaire. *Corporate Communications: An International Journal*, *26*(3), 589–604. https://doi.org/10.1108/CCIJ-01-2021-0006

Tsai, M., Chuang, S., & Hsieh, W. (2009). An integrated process model of communication satisfaction and organizational outcomes. *Social Behavior and Personality: An International Journal*, *37*(6), 825–834. https://doi.org/10.2224/sbp.2009.37.6.825

Varona, F. (1996). Relationship between communication satisfaction and organizational commitment in three Guatemalan organizations. *The Journal of Business Communication (1973)*, *33*(2), 111–140. https://doi.org/10.1177/002194369603300203

Yamaguchi, I. (2017). Instruments for organizational communication assessment for Japanese care facilities. *Corporate Communications: An International Journal*, *22*(4), 471–485. https://doi.org/10.1108/CCIJ-04-2017-0045

7 Employee engagement

Engagement is becoming an increasingly popular construct among practitioners and academics, leading to a growing body of research in different fields. However, the definitions and operationalizations of engagement remain inconsistent (Macey & Schneider, 2008), which is why there continues to be debate around how it differs conceptually and empirically from other constructs. In the research project from which this book emerged, we wanted to compare engagement against other constructs for predicting behavior, and we wanted to explore how engagement relates to internal communication.

Why engagement matters

Wefald and Downey (2009) asked whether job engagement is a fad, fashion, or folderol, "or does it deserve to be seen as a legitimate psychological construct leading to important organizational outcomes?" (p. 141). Legitimate or not, measuring engagement has appeal because it appears to contribute to bottom-line organizational performance (Macey & Schneider, 2008). Nevertheless, whether engagement is empirically different from other constructs is unclear (Christian et al., 2011). This is an important to explore because if engagement really contributes to outcomes of concern to management (Macey & Schneider, 2008), increasing employee engagement could give an organization a competitive advantage, especially as the nature of work is changing and as the workforce ages (Erickson, 2005).

Perhaps the most commonly used conceptualization of engagement is that of Gallup, which defined it as "an individual's involvement, satisfaction, and enthusiasm for work where people are emotionally connected to others at work and are cognitively vigilant" (Wefald & Downey, 2009, p. 142). Kahn (1990) defined engagement as "the simultaneous employment and expression of a person's 'preferred self' in task-related behaviors that promote connections to work and to others, personal presence (physical, cognitive, and emotional) and active, full

DOI: 10.4324/9781003200109-7

performances" (p. 700). He approached engagement as employees' willingness to invest themselves physically, cognitively, and emotionally in work roles. Engagement has also been defined as emotional and intellectual commitment to the organization (Baumruk, 2004; Shaw, 2005); an "individual's involvement and satisfaction with, as well as enthusiasm for work" (Harter et al., 2002, p. 417); or the amount of effort that an employee invests in his or her job (Frank et al., 2004). Many definitions approach engagement as something that employees bring to the workplace and that can lead to higher customer satisfaction, loyalty, productivity, and profit. According to Harter et al. (2002), all employees have the potential to be engaged.

Operationalizing engagement is challenging given that it has been described variously as a psychological state, performance construct, disposition, or combination of these (Macey & Schneider, 2008). Macey and Schneider (2008) differentiate *state engagement*, which is associated with job and work setting and which manifests as feelings of persistence, vigor, energy, dedication, absorption, enthusiasm, alertness, and pride; *behavioral engagement*, which is adaptive behavior that follows from state engagement; and trait engagement, which comprises several connected personality traits, such as positive affectivity, conscientiousness, proactive personality, and autotelic personality. Trait engagement can cause state engagement, and it indirectly influences behavioral engagement. Newman and Harrison (2008) have suggested that state engagement may not stand on its own as a concept but may simply reflect behavioral execution of a work role.

Disagreement about the definition of employee engagement complicates its measurement and management (Ferguson, 2007) as well as its comparison across studies. In our project, we defined engagement according to Schaufeli et al. (2002) as a positive, persistent, affective-motivational state of fulfillment, characterized by vigor, dedication, and absorption. Vigor is defined as "high levels of energy and mental resilience while working, the willingness to invest effort in one's work, and persistence even in the face of difficulties" (Schaufeli et al., 2006, p. 702). Dedication is defined as "being strongly involved in one's work and experiencing a sense of significance, enthusiasm, inspiration, pride, and challenge" (p. 702). Absorption is defined as "being fully concentrated and happily engrossed in one's work, whereby time passes quickly, and one has difficulties with detaching oneself from work" (p. 702).

While we began with an open mind about whether engagement is an attitude, motivational state, or personality trait, we ultimately decided to regard it as a psychological state involving certain behavioral expression (Bakker et al., 2014; Tkalac Verčič et al., 2021). This implies that engagement can be affected by internal communication, whereas if engagement is treated as a trait or aspect of personality, it should be less malleable to intervention (Welch, 2011).

Engagement in public relations

Slater et al. (1992) first introduced engagement in public relations by linking it to cognitive involvement and behavioral outcomes (Johnston, 2014). Since then, engagement has emerged as an important concept in public relations, with impacts on dialogue, social capital, and the organization-public relationship (Men & Tsai, 2014; Taylor & Kent, 2014). Engagement has also been linked to community building and different types of relationships (Johnston, 2014). In fact, Edelman (2008) has proposed renaming public relations as public engagement.

In this spirit, we edited a special issue of *Public Relations Review* on "Public Relations and Engagement" (Verčič et al., 2017), in which Jelen-Sanchez (2017) identified 58 publications on engagement in four major journals of public relations. This growing literature has focused on different types of engagement (Avidar, 2017). Dhanesh (2017) divided engagement in public relations into three types: social or digital media engagement, public or stakeholder engagement, and employee engagement. In public relations, most studies center on digital or social engagement (Jelen-Sanchez, 2017), such as through descriptions of how organizations interact with their publics through social media (Dhanesh, 2017). Engagement has also been examined in the context of corporate social responsibility (Lane & Devin, 2018), social businesses (Avidar, 2017), social capital (Johnston, 2018), and community engagement (Johnston & Lane, 2018). Engagement with the media has been explored as a potential antecedent to attitudinal and behavioral responses to mediated messages (Calder et al., 2009).

In public relations, engagement has been conceptualized as social interaction between organizations and their various stakeholders (Everett, 2018), or other types of participation and involvement at the level of the individual, organization, or society (Johnston, 2018). Taylor and Kent (2014) emphasized that "engagement is part of dialogue, and through engagement, organizations and publics can make decisions that create social capital" (p. 384). Indeed, engagement has been associated with interactivity and digital dialogic communication, such as in the form of comments and retweets (Men & Tsai, 2016; Morehouse & Saffer, 2019). This constitutes public engagement within the relationship approach to public relations research (Huang et al., 2021), which emphasizes communication as a process of creating meaning between organizations and their publics (Johnston, 2014). In this sense, public engagement has been approached as a communicative process (Shen & Sha, 2020; Taylor & Kent, 2014), whose purpose can range from manipulation to sense-making in order to build stakeholder relationships through dialogue (Kang & Kim, 2015). Another approach to public engagement focuses on affective quality, while some authors highlight behavioral aspects, such as in the context of strategic management (Dhanesh, 2017; Shen & Sha, 2020). In their study of alumni engagement, Shen and Sha (2020) try to reconcile different conceptualizations of public engagement, concluding that it comprises instrumental, communicative, and affective dimensions.

While this literature illustrates that engagement has been researched from diverse perspectives, existing research has been oriented mostly toward how engagement brings benefits to organizations (Ni et al., 2021), not how engagement can benefit other stakeholders or how it interacts with the cultural values of specific publics.

Employee engagement

While a rich literature exists on engagement in public relations, even more research has focused on employee engagement. In this research, engagement has traditionally been conceptualized based on theories of organizational behavior and psychology. Most studies have examined employees' engagement with their job, while some have analyzed their engagement with their organizations (Saks et al., 2022). Indeed, employees can be engaged with their role in a particular job position and engaged as a member of the larger organization (Saks, 2006).

Studies on employee engagement frequently explore potential antecedents (such as internal communication) and consequents (such as organizational commitment) (Mishra et al., 2014; Tkalac Verčič & Pološki Vokić, 2017; Welch, 2011). Christian et al. (2011) identified several factors positively related to engagement, including certain job characteristics, job complexity, transformational leadership, problem solving, social support, and exchange between leaders and members. They also identified factors such as work conditions and physical demands that are negatively related to engagement. Engagement shows a positive association with job satisfaction and organizational commitment (Saks, 2006), as well as job performance and organizational citizen behavior (Bakker & Bal, 2010). Conversely, engagement shows a negative association with staff turnover intention (Bailey et al., 2017).

Newman and Harrison (2008), commenting on work by Macey and Schneider (2008), suggest that engagement conceptually overlaps with affective components of job satisfaction. Newman and Harrison propose that nearly every UWES item parallels a similar item from scales measuring job satisfaction, job involvement, positive affect, or organizational commitment. Their assumption is that engagement represents a higher-order construct composed of several other constructs that correlate moderately or strongly with one another and whose definitions overlap.

The role of internal communication in employee engagement: general considerations

In most studies on employee engagement, communication is treated as an antecedent that can increase employee engagement (Pugh & Dietz, 2008; Wiley et al., 2010). For example, Welch (2011) proposed a model in which communication can strengthen employee engagement and implied organizational commitment. Similarly, we found that ICS was significantly related to employee engagement (Tkalac Verčič & Pološki Vokić, 2017), which is consistent with Ruck and Welch's (2012) conclusion that employee engagement is influenced by internal communication. Karanges et al. (2015) found that an employee's communication with his or her supervisor and, more generally, with the organization plays a significant role in developing and maintaining employee engagement, probably by facilitating interaction among organizations, supervisors, and employees and by creating workplace relationships. Iyer and Israel (2012) found a positive link between communication satisfaction and employee engagement. Several scholars see internal communication as one of the key determinants of employee engagement (Pugh & Dietz, 2008; Welch, 2011; Wiley et al., 2010). Studies of the relationship between internal communication and positive outcomes for individuals and organizations support this view (Karanges, 2014).

Ruck and Welch (2012) theorize that when supervisors communicate with their employees daily, they facilitate relational exchange. Therefore, the relationship between internal communication and employee engagement can be viewed in the framework of social exchange, according to which employees' feel obligated to return the benefits they receive (Karanges et al., 2015; Saks, 2006). Following the same idea, Duck (1994) positioned internal communication as a fundamental element of all exchange relationships.

Social exchanges involve an initiating action, a relationship between parties, and a reciprocity response (Cropanzano et al., 2017). The first step in social exchange occurs when the organization treats an employee positively or negatively. In response to positive actions, employees develop positive attitudes about the quality of the social exchange and actively provide positive responses. A succession of such positive exchanges between the organization and employee transforms an economic relationship into a relationship of high-quality social exchange.

The role of internal communication in employee engagement: our study

In the research project from which this book emerged, we relied on social exchange theory to explore ICS and workplace attitudes. We wanted to test whether ICS correlates with employees' perceptions of social exchange indicators and, in turn, employee engagement. We assumed that social exchange starts with internal communication (Tkalac Verčič et al., 2021); in other words, internal communication is the initiating action affecting social exchange between the organization and the employee. We hypothesized that higher ICS would correlate with a more positive opinion about the employee-employer relationship.

Using data from 3,457 employees in 26 domestic and international organizations in Croatia (see Chapter 6), we measured employee engagement using the Utrecht Work Engagement Scale (UWES), which has been validated multiple times (Bakker & Demerouti, 2008). Whether the concept has the three-dimensional structure stipulated on the UWES – or even a multidimensional structure at all – remains unclear. Some studies do support a three-dimensional structure (Hallberg & Schaufeli, 2006; Schaufeli & Bakker, 2004). Employees responded to items such as "At my work, I feel bursting with energy" and "I am enthusiastic about my job" using a Likert-type scale from 1 ("never") to 7 ("always"). Cronbach's alpha for this scale was .95, the mean was 4.98, and the standard deviation was 1.18.

Among the UWES items, those receiving the highest ratings were "At my work I always persevere, even when things do not go well" (mean 5.76) and "Time flies when I'm working" (mean 5.70), while the item receiving the lowest rating was "It's difficult to detach myself from my job" (mean 3.95) (Figure 7.1). This last item was the only item to be rated below 4. When we compared data collected from before the COVID-19 pandemic to data collected during the pandemic, we found that ratings on vigor and dedication increased slightly, while ratings on absorption decreased slightly (Figure 7.2).

These findings may have interesting implications for a work environment that has been transformed by the COVID-19 pandemic: we found that

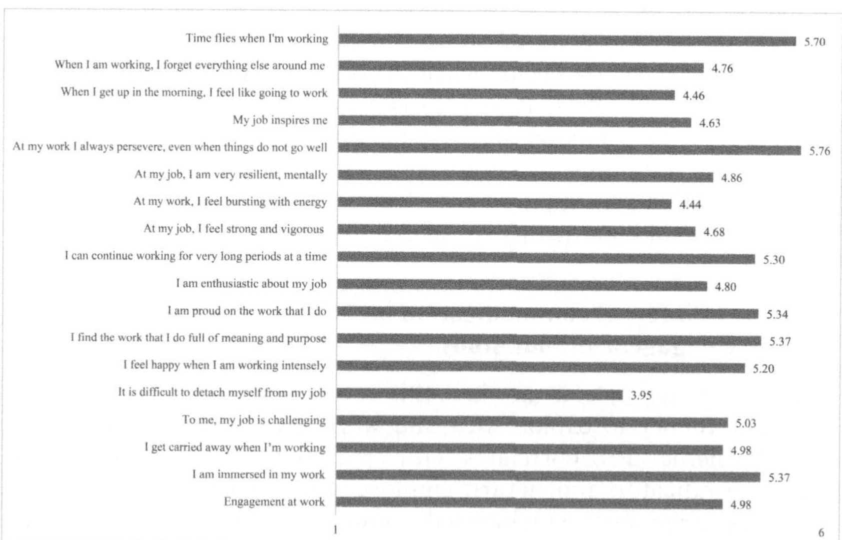

Figure 7.1 Mean ratings on the various UWES items on employee engagement ($N = 3{,}457$). Data collected before and during the COVID-19 pandemic were pooled.

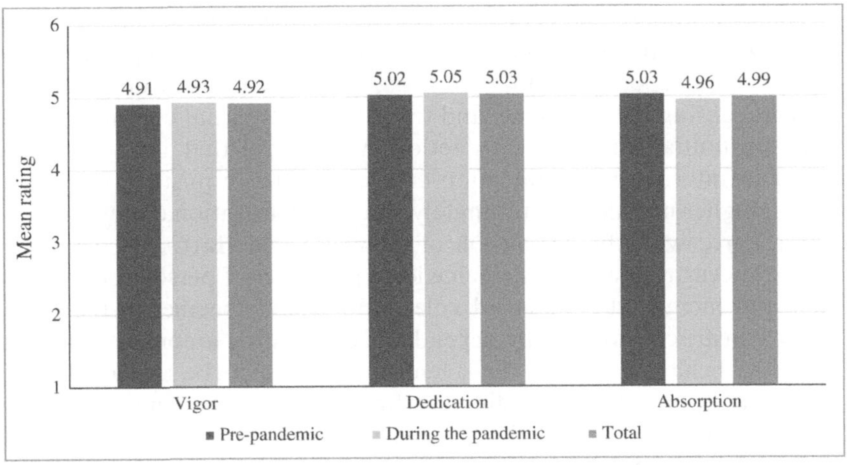

Figure 7.2 Mean ratings for the three dimensions of employee engagement on the UWES, stratified by whether data were collected before the COVID-19 pandemic ($N = 1{,}805$) or during the pandemic ($N = 1{,}652$). Also shown are the results for the entire sample, pooled together ("Total").

although engagement fell slightly during the pandemic, ICS increased. Our results are supported by other studies showing a decrease in engagement during the pandemic. The reason for this drop in engagement, according to Moyo et al. (2020), is fear of the risks associated with COVID-19, including health issues and even death. Song et al. (2021) recorded a decrease in engagement but an increase in job satisfaction among workers returning to their workplaces after lockdown. Ferdian et al. (2021), in contrast, observed a decrease not only in engagement, but also in motivation and job satisfaction. Stressful events can increase exhaustion while decreasing coping resources, which in turn renders employees more passive and less engaged (Eatough et al., 2012). Our research project supports the idea that the pandemic has led to organizational changes that have created ambiguity and stress, in turn reducing employee engagement.

In contrast to engagement, ICS improved during the pandemic, which demonstrates that timely and transparent communication can increase satisfaction among employees. This is further evidence that employee attitudes toward the organization are affected by how management communicates (Koronis & Ponis, 2018). Organizational crises create substantial uncertainty, so organizations should highlight truth, accuracy, and transparency when communicating with their employees (Johansen et al., 2012). The COVID-19 pandemic has led organizations to pay more attention to their internal communication and has forced them to communicate transparently. During crises, they look for guidance and support, so a greater communication effort from the organization can increase communication satisfaction.

Understanding how crises affect engagement is important because organizations are increasingly striving to engage their employees. The available evidence, including from our research project, demonstrates how increasing the frequency and timeliness of internal communication can substantially impact satisfaction. We believe that investing more effort in internal communication can lead to more positive work attitudes, higher morale and, ultimately, better organizational outcomes.

We agree with the conclusion of Newman and Harrison (2008) that employee engagement is "the behavioral provision of personal resources, time and energy, into one's work role, and it can be specified as the higher order construct indicated by dependable covariation among several, valued work behaviors" (p. 35). Engagement can therefore be seen as a higher-order behavioral construct different from job attitudes and personality traits. From this we conclude that employee engagement and ICS can be treated as two separate constructs. In our study, overall ICS and all ICS dimensions showed significant positive relationships with employee engagement as well as all three dimensions of individual engagement. The relationship between satisfaction with feedback and employee engagement was the strongest. Satisfaction with feedback was significantly related to all three engagement dimensions, while satisfaction with informal communication added to the explanation of employee absorption and vigor. These results are in line with our previous work (Tkalac Verčič & Pološki Vokić, 2017).

Conclusion

Internal communication is considered an antecedent that can increase employee engagement (Pugh & Dietz, 2008; Wiley et al., 2010). Tkalac Verčič and Pološki Vokić (2017) found that higher ICS correlated with greater employee engagement, which reflects Ruck and Welch's (2012) conclusion that internal corporate communication can influence employee engagement. Our research, together with a growing literature, supports the idea that clear two-way communication and effective communication procedures can increase the engagement of employees and improve their regard for their employer.

References

Avidar, R. (2017). Public relations and social businesses: The importance of enhancing engagement. *Public Relations Review*, *43*(5), 955–962. https://doi.org/10.1016/j.pubrev.2017.03.015

Bailey, C., Madden, A., Alfes, K., & Fletcher, L. (2017). The meaning, antecedents and outcomes of employee engagement: A narrative synthesis. *International Journal of Management Reviews*, *19*(1), 31–53. https://doi.org/10.1111/ijmr.12077

Bakker, A. B., & Bal, M. P. (2010). Weekly work engagement and performance: A study among starting teachers. *Journal of Occupational and Organizational Psychology*, *83*(1), 189–206. https://doi.org/10.1348/096317909X402596

Bakker, A. B., & Demerouti, E. (2008). Towards a model of work engagement. *Career Development International*, *13*(3), 209–223. https://doi.org/10.1108/13620430810870476

Bakker, A. B., Demerouti, E., & Sanz-Vergel, A. I. (2014). Burnout and work engagement: The JD–R approach. *Annual Review of Organizational Psychology and Organizational Behavior*, *1*, 389–411. https://doi.org/10.1146/annurev-orgpsych-031413-091235

Baumruk, R. (2004). The missing link: The role of employee engagement in business success. *Workspan*, *47*(1), 48–52.

Calder, B. J., Malthouse, E. C., & Schaedel, U. (2009). An experimental study of the relationship between online engagement and advertising effectiveness. *Journal of Interactive Marketing*, *23*(4), 321–331. https://doi.org/10.1016/j.intmar.2009.07.002

Christian, M. S., Garza, A. S., & Slaughter, J. E. (2011). Work engagement: A quantitative review and test of its relations with task and contextual performance. *Personnel Psychology*, *64*(1), 89–136. https://doi.org/10.1111/j.1744-6570.2010.01203.x

Cropanzano, R., Anthony, E. L., Daniels, S. R., & Hall, A. V. (2017). Social exchange theory: A critical review with theoretical remedies. *Academy of Management Annals*, *11*(1), 479–516. https://doi.org/doi.org/10.5465/annals.2015.0099

Dhanesh, G. S. (2017). Putting engagement in its proper place: State of the field, definition and model of engagement in public relations. *Public Relations Review*, *43*(5), 925–933. https://doi.org/10.1016/j.pubrev.2017.04.001

Duck, S. (1994). *Meaningful relationships: Talking, sense, and relating*. Thousand Oaks, CA: Sage Publications.

Eatough, E. M., Way, J. D., & Chang, C. H. (2012). Understanding the link between psychosocial work stressors and work-related musculoskeletal complaints. *Applied Ergonomics*, *43*(3), 554–563. https://doi.org/10.1016/j.apergo.2011.08.009

Edelman, R. (2008). *Edelman trust barometer*. Retrieved from http://www.edelman.com/p/6-a-m/2008-edelman-trust-barometer/

Erickson, T. J. (2005, May 26). Testimony submitted before the U.S. Senate Committee on Health, Education, Labor and Pensions. https://www.govinfo.gov/content/pkg/CHRG-109shrg21585/html/CHRG-109shrg21585.htm

Everett, J. (2018). Toward a cultural ecology of engagement. In K. A. Johnston, & M. Taylor (Eds.), *The handbook of communication engagement* (pp. 91–102). Wiley.

Ferdian, A., Azis, E., Prasetio, A. P., & Darmawan, M. I. (2021). Human resources practice and employee engagement: The mediation of organizational support and employee satisfaction. *European Journal of Molecular & Clinical Medicine*, *7*(10), 1576–1590.

Ferguson, A. (2007). *Employee engagement: Does it exist, and if so, how does it relate to performance, other constructs and individual differences?* Retrieved from http://www.lifethatworks.com/Employee-Engagement.prn.pdf

Frank, F. D., Finnegan, R. P., & Taylor, C. R. (2004). The race for talent: Retaining and engaging workers in the 21st century. *Human Resource Planning*, *27*(3), 12–25. Retrieved from http://webcache.googleusercontent.com/search

Hallberg, U., & Schaufeli, W. B. (2006). "Same same" but different? – Can work engagement be discriminated from job involvement and organizational commitment? *European Psychologist*, *11*(2), 119–127. https://doi.org/10.1027/1016-9040.11.2.119

Harter, J. K., Schmidt, F. L., & Hayes, T. L. (2002). Business-unit level relationship between employee satisfaction, employee engagement, and business outcomes: A meta-analysis. *Journal of Applied Psychology*, *87*(2), 268–279.

Huang, Q., Jin, J., Lynn, B. J., & Men, L. R. (2021). Relationship cultivation and public engagement via social media during the covid-19 pandemic in China. *Public Relations Review*, *47*(4), 102064. https://doi.org/10.1016/j.pubrev.2021.102064

Iyer, S., & Israel, D. (2012). Structural equation modeling for testing the impact of organization communication satisfaction on employee engagement. *South Asian Journal of Management*, *19*(1), 51–81.

Jelen-Sanchez, A. (2017). Engagement in public relations discipline: Themes, theoretical perspectives and methodological approaches. *Public Relations Review*, *43*(5), 934–944. https://doi.org/10.1016/j.pubrev.2017.04.002

Johansen, W., Aggerholm, H. K., & Frandsen, F. (2012). Entering new territory: A study of internal crisis management and crisis communication in organizations. *Public Relations Review*, *38*(2), 270–279. https://doi.org/10.1016/j.pubrev.2011.11.0

Johnston, K. A. (2014). Public relations and engagement: Theoretical imperatives of a multidimensional concept. *Journal of Public Relations Research*, *26*(5), 381–383. https://doi.org/10.1080/1062726X.2014.959863

Johnston, K. A. (2018). Toward a theory of social engagement. In K. A. Johnston, & M. Taylor (Eds.), *The handbook of communication engagement* (pp. 19–32). John Wiley & Sons.

Johnston, K. A., & Lane, A. B. (2018). Building relational capital: The contribution of episodic and relational community engagement. *Public Relations Review*, *44*(5), 633–644. https://doi.org/10.1016/j.pubrev.2018.10.006

Kahn, W. A. (1990). Psychological conditions of personal engagement and disengagement at work. *Academy of Management Journal*, *33*(4), 692–724. https://doi.org/10.5465/256287

Kang, J., & Kim, J. (2015, May). Family business and firm value: evidence from stakeholder relations with employees. Asian Bureau of Finance and Economic Research Conference, Singapore. Retrieved from http://abfer.org/media/abfer-events-2015/annual-conference/corporate-finance/family-business-and-firm-value-evidence-from-stakeholder-relations-with-employees.pdf

Karanges, E., Johnston, K., Beatson, A., & Lings, I. (2015). The influence of internal communication on employee engagement: A pilot study. *Public Relations Review*, *41*(1), 129–131. https://doi.org/10.1016/j.pubrev.2014.12.003

Karanges, E. R. (2014). *Optimising Employee Engagement with Internal Communication: A Social Exchange Perspective* [Master's thesis, Queensland University of Technology, Brisbane]. https://eprints.qut.edu.au/71024/

Koronis, E., & Ponis, S. (2018). A strategic approach to crisis management and organizational resilience. *Journal of Business Strategy*, *39*(1), 32–42. https://doi.org/10.1108/JBS-10-2016-0124

Lane, A. B., & Devin, B. (2018). Operationalizing stakeholder engagement in CSR: A process approach. *Corporate Social Responsibility and Environmental Management*, *25*(3), 267–280. https://doi.org/10.1002/csr.1460

Macey, W. H., & Schneider, B. (2008). The meaning of employee engagement. *Industrial and Organizational Psychology*, *1*(1), 3–30. https://doi.org/10.1111/j.1754-9434.2007.0002.x

Men, L. R., & Tsai, W. H. S. (2014). Perceptual, attitudinal, and behavioral outcomes of organization–public engagement on corporate social networking sites. *Journal of Public Relations Research*, *26*(5), 417–435. https://doi.org/10.1080/1062726X.2014.951047

Men, L. R., & Tsai, W. H. S. (2016). Public engagement with CEOs on social media: Motivations and relational outcomes. *Public Relations Review*, *42*(5), 932–942. https://doi.org/10.1016/j.pubrev.2016.08.001

Mishra, K., Boynton, L., & Mishra, A. (2014). Driving employee engagement: The expanded role of internal communications. *Journal of Business Communication*, *51*(2), 183–202. https://doi.org/10.1177/2329488414525399

Morehouse, J., & Saffer, A. J. (2019). Illuminating the invisible college: An analysis of foundational and prominent publications of engagement research in public relations. *Public Relations Review*, *45*(5), 101836. https://doi.org/10.1016/j.pubrev.2019.101836

Moyo, T., Duffett, R., & Knott, B. (2020). Environmental factors and stakeholders influence on professional sport organisations engagement in sustainable corporate social responsibility: A South African perspective. *Sustainability*, *12*(11), 4504. https://doi.org/10.3390/su12114504

Newman, D. A., & Harrison, D. A. (2008). Been there, bottled that: Are state and behavioural work engagement new and useful construct 'wines'? *Industrial and Organisational Psychology*, *1*, 31–35. https://doi.org/10.1111/j.1754-9434.2007.00003.x

Ni, L., De la Flor, M., Wang, Q., & Romero, V. (2021). Engagement in context: Making meaning of the Latino community health engagement process. *Public Relations Review*, *47*(2), 102036. https://doi.org/10.1016/j.pubrev.2021.102036

Pugh, S. D., & Dietz, J. (2008). Employee engagement at the organizational level of analysis. *Industrial and Organizational Psychology*, *1*(1), 45–48. https://doi.org/10.1111/j.1754-9434.2007.00006.x

Ruck, K., & Welch, M. (2012). Valuing internal communication: Management and employee perspective. *Public Relations Review*, *38*(2), 294–302. https://doi.org/10.1016/j.pubrev.2011.12.016

Saks, A. M. (2006). Antecedents and consequences of employee engagement. *Journal of Managerial Psychology*, *21*(7), 600–619. https://doi.org/10.1108/02683940610690169

Saks, A. M., Gruman, J. A., & Zhang, Q. (2022). Organization engagement: A review and comparison to job engagement. *Journal of Organizational Effectiveness: People and Performance*, *9*(1), 20–49. https://doi.org/10.1108/JOEPP-12-2020-0253

Schaufeli, W. B., & Bakker, A. B. (2004). Job demands, job resources, and their relationship with burnout and engagement: A multi-sample study. *Journal of Organizational Behavior*, *25*(3), 293–315. https://doi.org/10.1002/job.248

Schaufeli, W. B., Bakker, A. B., & Salanova, M. (2006). The measurement of work engagement with a short questionnaire a cross-national study. *Educational and Psychological Measurement*, *66*(4), 701–716. https://doi.org/10.1177/0013164405282471

Schaufeli, W. B., Salanova, M., González-Romá, V., & Bakker, A. B. (2002). The measurement of engagement and burnout: A two sample confirmatory factor analytic approach. *Journal of Happiness Studies*, *3*(1), 71–92. https://doi.org/10.1023/A:1015630930326

Shaw, K. (2005). An engagement strategy process for communicators. *Strategic Communication Management*, *9*(3), 26–29.

Shen, H., & Sha, B. L. (2020). Conceptualizing and operationalizing alumni engagement: When conversational voice matters more than openness and assurances of legitimacy. *Public Relations Review*, *46*(5), 101974. https://doi.org/10.1016/j.pubrev.2020.101974

Slater, M. D., Chipman, H., Auld, G., Keefe, T., & Kendall, P. (1992). Information processing and situational theory: A cognitive response analysis. *Journal of Public Relations Research*, *4*(4), 189–203. https://doi.org/10.1207/s1532754xjprr0404_1

Song, L., Wang, Y., & Zhao, Y. (2021). How employee authenticity shapes work attitudes and behaviors: The mediating role of psychological capital and the moderating role of leader authenticity. *Journal of Business and Psychology*, *36*, 1125–1136. https://doi.org/10.1007/s10869-020-09725-0

Taylor, M., & Kent, M. L. (2014). Dialogic engagement: Clarifying foundational concepts. *Journal of Public Relations Research*, *26*(5), 384–398. https://doi.org/10.1080/1062726X.2014.956106

Tkalac Verčič, A., & Pološki Vokić, N. (2017). Engaging employees through internal communication. *Public Relations Review*, *43*(5), 885–893. https://doi.org/10.1016/j.pubrev.2017.04.005

Tkalac Verčič, A., Galić, Z., & Žnidar, K. (2021). The relationship of internal communication satisfaction with employee engagement and employer attractiveness: Testing the joint mediating effect of the social exchange quality indicators [Advanced online publication]. *International Journal of Business Communication*. https://doi.org/10.1177/23294884211053839

Verčič, D., Tkalac Verčič, A., & Sriramesh, K. (2017). Editorial: Special section on engagement (based on the 23rd International Public relations Research Symposium—BledCom). *Public Relations Review*, *43*(5), 883–884. https://doi.org/10.1016/j.pubrev.2017.08.002

Wefald, A. J., & Downey, R. G. (2009). Job engagement in organizations: Fad, fashion, or folderol? *Journal of Organizational Behavior: The International Journal of Industrial, Occupational and Organizational Psychology and Behavior*, *30*(1), 141–145. https://doi.org/10.1002/job.560

Welch, M. (2011). The evolution of the employee engagement concept: Communication implications. *Corporate Communications: An International Journal*, *16*(4), 328–346. https://doi.org/10.1108/13563281111186968

Wiley, J. W., Kowske, B. J., & Herman, A. E. (2010). Developing and validating a global model of employee engagement. In S. L. Albrecht (Ed.), *Handbook of employee engagement: Perspectives, issues, research and practice* (pp. 351–363). Edward Elgar. https://doi.org/10.4337/9781849806374.00039

8 Employer branding

An employer brand can bring crucial advantages to an organization, which makes the concept relevant to academics and practitioners, especially in the fields of communication, marketing, and human resources management. Essentially, an employer brand is what differentiates one organization as employer from other organizations. As part of the research project from which this book emerged, we measured employer attractiveness among organization's employees and explored relationships of this attractiveness with internal communication. In this chapter we will try to demonstrate the importance of an efficient employer brand, identifying some advantages it creates for an organization and defining how communication influences it.

What brands mean in general and for an employer

Brands are the sum of all properties, benefits, and values that a specific object provides, as perceived by individuals (Kotler, 1997), and that therefore differentiate that object from other, similar objects. These perceived associations constitute "promises" based on trust, consistency, and expectations in order to occupy a unique position in an individual's mind (Davis, 2000). The most common type of brands is product brands. A product brand is the intangible part of the product (Levitt, 1980) that is a symbolic representation of the product itself, which gives it characteristics and a personality (Gardner & Levy, 1955), differentiating it from other similar products.

Analogously, an employer brand, first defined by Ambler and Barrow (1996), is "the package of functional, economic and psychological benefits provided by employment, and identified with the employing company" (p. 187). Employer brands constitute promises about an individual's experience as an employee at that company (Backhaus, 2016), differentiating that organization as an employer from other organizations (Backhaus & Tikoo, 2004). In other words, the employer brand is the perception of what an organization can offer as an employer in the minds of past, current, and potential employees (Rampl & Kenning, 2014). Just as with product

DOI: 10.4324/9781003200109-8

brands, attributes linked to an employer brand create a set of traits akin to a personality (Lievens & Highhouse, 2003), designed to create a positive perception of an employer (Ambler & Barrow, 1996). A brand is what makes an organization human, while an employer brand is what makes an employer human (Davies, 2008).

If branding is the sum of all activities that differentiate, create loyalty, ensure satisfaction, and create emotional engagement with the product (Davies, 2008), then employer branding is a process of creating, communicating, and delivering promises and real experiences to the employee – the so-called employment offer. This offer constitutes "the envisioned benefits that a potential employee sees in working for a specific organisation" (Berthon et al., 2005, p. 156). Organizations can promise various types of benefits to employees, including an environment that supports professional development through educational activities; material and financial rewards; and feelings of being valued and involved (Ambler & Barrow, 1996). As Sartain and Schumann (2006) emphasize, employer branding arises through the collaboration of three corporate functions: marketing, human resources, and corporate communications.

Internal and external employer brands

Efforts at employer branding that target current employees can be considered internal employer branding, while efforts that target potential employees can be considered external employer branding. According to Backhaus and Tikoo (2004), the two types of branding efforts arise through a three-step process. First, an employment offer is created within the organization; second, that offer is marketed toward potential employees; and third, the offer is implemented within the organization through internal employer branding. The goal of this process is to create attraction (external employer branding) and commitment (internal employer branding) (Backhaus, 2016; Backhaus & Tikoo, 2004). In other words, the perception of external employer brands is the perception of what employers promise to deliver, while internal employer brands are what employers actually deliver (Backhaus, 2016). In another formulation, Lievens and Slaughter (2016) equated external employer brands with the image that organizations create in order to be considered desirable employers, while internal employer brands are the identity of an organization. The ideal situation is when external and internal employer brands are the same: this means that employees' expectations are fulfilled. In addition, such alignment makes it more likely that current and potential employees will have a positive perception of the organization (Gioia et al., 2000).

In this sense, employees can be considered as "corporate ambassadors and brand advocates that represent the organization to external stakeholders" (Men, 2014, p. 265). Employees can endorse their employer's brand through so-called "employee branding" (Backhaus, 2018), which occurs through internal marketing that seeks to fulfill employees' expectations and create a motivational organizational culture that builds satisfaction (Miles & Mangold, 2004); as well as through the internalization of the employer brand by current employees, such that they will promote the brand to potential employees (Cervellon & Lirio, 2017; Keeling et al., 2013). In other words, employer brand perception is created internally and projected externally by current employees to desired employees.

Becoming an employer of choice

One of the key objectives in developing and managing an employer brand is to become an attractive employer to desired employees, whether current or future. The perception of an employer as attractive generates many benefits for the organization. One is stronger brand equity (Berthon et al., 2005; Cable & Turban, 2003), which refers to how valuable the brand itself is for the organization in differentiating it from other brands (Keller, 1993). Strong brand equity can make potential employees more willing to join the organization, even if it means paying "a premium in the form of lower wages" (Cable & Turban, 2003, p. 2245), which the same individuals may not feel toward other employer brands.

Thus, strong brand equity can help organizations attract and retain desired employees (Barrow & Mosley, 2005), which may be related to various attributes of the employer (Chinsky Matuson, 2013). One of these attributes is whether the employer's perceived value system aligns with that of desired employees (Cable & Judge, 1994; Chatman, 1989, 1991). This means that employers should aim to support the value system of the desired pool of employees. At the same time, the organization can adjust its "personality" by adopting characteristics attractive to desired employees, including a certain organizational culture, organizational values, workforce diversity, business strategy, and willingness to pay a competitive salary (Rynes & Barber, 1990). Other characteristics include organizational structure (Turban & Keon, 1993) and reward systems (Bretz et al., 1989). Organizations should avail themselves of all these factors in order to create and deliver a strong employment offer (Keller & Meaney, 2017).

Employer brand equity positively affects employees' well-being, making them more loyal to their employer and weakening their intent to leave (Ambler & Barrow, 1996; Backhaus & Tikoo, 2004; Benraiss-Noailles & Viot, 2021; Heilmann et al., 2013). Loyal employees have a strong bond with their employer, which arises from a sense of purpose and creates satisfaction (Logan, 1984). High employee satisfaction leads, in turn, to higher job satisfaction (Terera & Ngirande, 2014), employee engagement (Tkalac Verčič et al., 2021b), employee performance (Iaffaldano & Muchinsky, 1985), and customer satisfaction (Morrison, 1996; Schmit & Allscheid, 1995).

The benefits of greater employer attractiveness for the satisfaction, performance, and retention of individual employees translate to better systemic outcomes for the organization as a whole. Human resources processes, including recruitment, run more smoothly, cost less and can be more flexible, in part because employees are less likely to abuse sick leave (Heilmann et al., 2013). Relationships among employees and between employees and organization (employee-organization relationships) are stronger, leading to a more powerful organizational culture (Ambler & Barrow, 1996; Backhaus & Tikoo, 2004), and corporate brand (Foster et al., 2010; Tkalac Verčič & Sinčić Ćorić, 2018). Ultimately, all this can create a significant competitive advantage for the organization, improving profits (Backhaus & Tikoo, 2004; Barrow & Mosley, 2005; Heilmann et al., 2013; Love & Singh, 2011).

Being simply an attractive employer brand may not, however, be enough in the "war on talents", in which organizations compete for desired employees. Instead, employers should strive to be an "employer of choice" to their desired employees (Elving et al., 2013; Rampl, 2014), i.e., "the most attractive employer brand" (Rampl et al., 2016, p. 365). Becoming the employer of choice must be achieved through emotional engagement (Rampl, 2014): factors that boost employer attractiveness, such as opportunities for professional advancement, work scope, organizational culture, and financial rewards, can help an organization become an employer of choice *only* if they encourage an emotional response. Rampl et al. (2016) confirmed this idea by using functional magnetic resonance imaging to show that emotional responses are triggered in the brain when individuals decide about their employer of choice.

Evaluating an employer brand: general considerations

Employer attractiveness is the result of employer branding, and these terms are often used interchangeably (Tkalac Verčič, 2021). As a result, most studies to evaluate employer brands rely on scales that examine the level of employer attractiveness. One of the most commonly used scales is the Employer Attractiveness Scale (EmpAt), which was developed by Berthon et al. (2005) and contains 25 items that measure the importance or attractiveness of a given benefit provided by the employer. Items measuring importance are directed at external publics, while those measuring presence are directed at internal publics. The 25 benefits reflect five values for employees (interest, social, economic, development, and application), with five items dedicated to each value. The interest value refers to the attractiveness of the organization's innovative tendencies; social value, the attractiveness of social relationships within the organization; economic value, the attractiveness of financial rewards offered by the organization; development value, the attractiveness of possibilities for professional and personal development; and application value, the attractiveness of corporate social responsibility and organizational support. The EmpAt has shown validity in numerous studies (e.g., Pološki

Vokić et al., 2021; Špoljarić & Tkalac Verčič, 2022; Tkalac Verčič, 2021; Tkalac Verčič & Sinčić Ćorić, 2018; Tkalac Verčič et al., 2021a).

Davies et al. (2004) developed a corporate character scale that can be used to measure employees' and customers' perception of an organization's reputation, making it useful for evaluating employer brands. This scale approaches an organization's corporate brand as its personality and measures to what extent certain personality traits are perceived as present by employees or customers. The scale comprises seven dimensions: *agreeableness* (13 items), which examines "human personality" in terms of warmth, empathy, and integrity; *enterprise* (9 items), which measures "extroversion" of an employer in terms of modernity, adventure, and boldness; *competence* (9 items), which assesses satisfaction with the organization in terms of conscientiousness, drive, and technocracy; *chic* (8 items), which describes the level of sophistication an organization's brand represents in terms of elegance, prestige, and snobbery; *ruthlessness* (6 items), which represents what brands do *not* wish to project and evaluates actual experience as opposed to perceived promises, in terms of egotism and dominance; *informality* (3 items); and *machismo* (3 items). These last two dimensions have been used in a few studies (Davies & Chun, 2002; Tkalac Verčič & Verčič, 2007) but not many others (e.g., Chun & Davies, 2006; Davies, 2008; Davies et al., 2018; Men & Sung, 2019; Men & Tsai, 2015). This scale has been used to assess overall corporate reputation based on an organization's image and identity. Thus, it is not a pure, direct measure of an employer's attractiveness. Nevertheless, it can reveal positive and negative aspects of an employer that do influence its attractiveness.

Highhouse et al. (2003) developed a scale to evaluate employer brands based on the three dimensions of *general organizational attractiveness,* which assesses an organization's attractiveness as an employer and as an organization more generally; *intention to pursue*, which measures to what extent the respondent would be willing to take action in order to become an employee of the organization; and *company prestige*, which measures an organization's "social influence, such as reputation, popularity, and status" (p. 992). Each dimension is covered by five items. According to their model, an organization's attractiveness and prestige influence intention to pursue. Considering the items in this scale, it can be used only to measure external employer brands. Lievens and Highhouse (2003) created another scale that assesses job likability and organizational "personality" traits, which can also be related to employer attractiveness.

Each of these scales has limitations. The EmpAt scale, for example, was developed using a student sample, which may help explain why the level of attractiveness cannot predict employer brand strength or an individual's willingness to pursue an employer. The corporate character scale, for its part, was designed to assess corporate reputation, not employer brands. Therefore, researchers who wish to apply it to employer brands must compare the measured perception with the perception that the organization intended to elicit. Even when the intended and actual perception align well, this still does not necessarily mean that an employer brand is strong enough to make an organization the "employer of choice" to its desired employees. In other words, researchers should know which personality traits the desired employees value the most if they wish to assess an employer brand using the corporate character scale. The scale developed by Highhouse et al. (2003) measures only external employer brand, which is only part of the overall employer brand. The scale developed by Lievens and Highhouse (2003) was created in a very specific environment: for assessing the employer brand of the Belgian army. This scale does not measure all aspects of employer brand, and it is culturally specific (Berthon et al., 2005). This falls under the scope of international, or global, employer branding. However, available studies on international employer branding are scarce and heterogeneous in their quality, such that the question of how to evaluate an international employer brand remains open.

Evaluating an employer brand: our study

In our EmpAt survey of 3,457 employees at 26 small, mid-size, and large Croatian organizations operating domestically or internationally, we found that respondents were most attracted by efforts of their employers to create social value (Figure 8.1) in the form of a supportive work environment in which they can have high-quality relationships with one another and with their superiors. The attractiveness of social value remained high during the COVID-19 pandemic began, signaling the continuing importance of their employers' ability and willingness to innovate in order to nurture a supportive work environment and organizational atmosphere, particularly

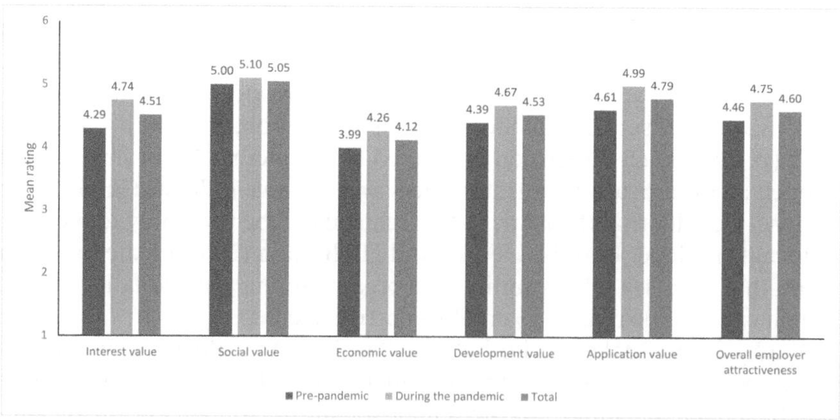

Figure 8.1 Dimensions of employer attractiveness, based on the EmpAt scale, in our study of 3,457 employees at 26 Croatian organizations stratified by whether data were collected before the COVID-19 pandemic ($N = 1,805$) or during the pandemic ($N = 1,652$). Also shown are the results for the entire sample, pooled together ("Total").

while drawing on the creativity of employees. The observation that the pandemic did not dampen the importance of social value likely reflects pandemic-induced innovation in internal marketing, such as intensification of digital internal communication in response to working from home.

We also found that economic value became more attractive after the pandemic began, although employees found their organizations to perform less well in this area than in other areas. Therefore, this increase in attractiveness should be investigated further: is it due to the fact that employers increased financial rewards, or did employees become more sympathetic to their employers and lower their financial expectations? Nevertheless, employees seem to find economic value the least attractive of all dimensions contributing to employer attractiveness.

Communicating employer brands: our study

When creating, developing, and managing an employer brand, employers should market it to internal and external publics using marketing communication, in order to ensure consistency among the internal and external channels (Moroko & Uncles, 2008). Internal communication, for its part, contributes to employee commitment, which in turn influences employer attractiveness (Barrow & Mosley, 2005). Thus, higher ICS should be associated with higher employer attractiveness. This association is indeed supported by our study, where all dimensions of ICS and employer attractiveness showed positive, significant relationships with one another (Tables 8.1 and 8.2). The ICS dimension of satisfaction with communication climate showed the strongest correlation with overall employer attractiveness, interest value, development value, and

Table 8.1 Matrix of correlations among dimensions of internal communication satisfaction (ICS) and employer attractiveness in our study

	EA	*IV*	*SV*	*EV*	*DV*	*AV*
ICS	.897**	.837**	.793**	.797**	.848**	.853**
SwF	.833**	.786**	.705**	.752**	.802**	.785**
SwIS	.741**	.664**	.705**	.645**	.710**	.688**
SwHC	.752**	.679**	.794**	.624**	.671**	.709**
SwIC	.790**	.732**	.718**	.708**	.741**	.738**
SwIO	.795**	.759**	.635**	.727**	.756**	.777**
SwCC	.837**	.793**	.713**	.740**	.805**	.800**
SwQM	.799**	.757**	.667**	.719**	.756**	.774**
SwCM	.790**	.740**	.687**	.708**	.744**	.756**

Legend: AV, application value; DV, development value; EV, economic value; EA, employer attractiveness; IV, interest value; SwCC, satisfaction with communication climate; SwCM, satisfaction with communication in meetings; SwF, satisfaction with feedback; SwHC, satisfaction with horizontal communication; SwIC, satisfaction with informal communication; SwIO, satisfaction with information about the organization; SwIS, satisfaction with communication with immediate superior; SwQM, satisfaction with the quality of communication media; SV, social value

** $p < .01$.

Table 8.2 Comparison of the 26 organizations in our study based on mean internal communication satisfaction (ICS) and employer attractiveness*

	ICS		*Employer Attractiveness*	
Organization	*M*	*Rank*	*M*	*Rank*
1	6.10	1	6.28	1
2	5.48	2	5.44	4
3	5.31	3	5.49	2
4	5.24	4	5.35	7
5	5.23	5	5.25	11
6	5.19	6	5.37	5
7	5.17	7	5.36	6
8	5.13	8	5.28	10
9	5.09	9	5.1	12
10	5.07	10	5.33	8
11	5.03	11	5.28	9
12	4.82	12	4.79	13
13	4.82	13	5.47	3
14	4.72	14	4.65	16
15	4.63	15	4.74	14
16	4.56	16	4.41	17
17	4.47	17	4.72	15
18	4.32	18	4.27	20
19	4.22	19	4.28	18
20	4.20	20	4.25	21
21	3.98	21	4.23	22
22	3.97	22	4.20	23
23	3.93	23	3.67	26
24	3.82	24	4.28	19
25	3.67	25	3.72	25
26	3.43	26	3.67	26

* Companies are listed according to their ICS rank.

application value. These results make sense given that this ICS dimension measures satisfaction with an organization's ability to promote the internalization of employer branding and to create a positive organizational atmosphere and positive image of the employer.

When we ranked the organizations in our study according to mean ICS and employer attractiveness, a general rule of thumb emerged: the higher ICS was, the greater employer attractiveness was (Table 8.2). This comes as no surprise, since satisfied employees perceive their employers as more attractive (Davies, 2008).

Conclusion

Employer brands represent the image that an organization develops and manages as an employer in order to attract desired employees, whether current or potential. Internal employer brands target current employees, while external employer brands target potential employees, and the two should be aligned in order to ensure internalization of the employer brand, leading to greater likelihood that individuals will pursue employment at the organization, as well as greater commitment and work satisfaction among those already working there (Backhaus, 2018). A strong, positive employer brand can increase employer attractiveness (Berthon et al., 2005), in turn building employer brand equity (Berthon et al., 2005; Cable & Turban, 2003) and improving the organization's ability to attract new talent (Barrow & Mosley, 2005) and retain current talent (Benraiss-Noailles & Viot, 2021). Ultimately, this creates a competitive advantage for the organization (Backhaus & Tikoo, 2004; Barrow & Mosley, 2005; Heilmann et al., 2013; Love & Singh, 2011).

A crucial part of employer branding is internal communication, since it supports the development and management of an internal employer brand, which is later communicated externally to potential employees. Of course, the internal and external brands should be consistent with each other. Another condition for branding success is that an employer brand create an emotional relationship with desired employees in order for the organization to become their employer of choice (Rampl, 2014; Rampl et al., 2016). Becoming an employer of choice should in fact be the ultimate goal of employer branding efforts.

Despite their importance to organizational success, employer brands remain difficult to evaluate quantitatively. Scales commonly used to evaluate it may assess only some dimensions, or they may assess employer attractiveness as a proxy. Future research should aim to create direct, rigorous scales of employer brands, preferably from local and international perspectives.

References

Ambler, T., & Barrow, S. (1996). The employer brand. *Journal of Brand Management*, *4*(3), 185–206. https://doi.org/10.1057/bm.1996.42

Backhaus, K. (2016). Employer branding revisited. *Organization Management Journal*, *13*(4), 193–201. https://doi.org/10.1080/15416518.2016.1245128

Backhaus, K. (2018). People make the brand: A commentary. *Management Research: Journal of the Iberoamerican Academy of Management*, *16*(4), 380–387. https://doi.org/10.1108/MRJIAM-12-2017-0800

Backhaus, K., & Tikoo, S. (2004). Conceptualizing and researching employer branding. *Career Development International*, *9*(5), 501–517. https://doi.org/10.1108/13620430410550754

Barrow, S., & Mosley, R. (2005). *The employer brand: Bringing the Best of brand management to people at work*. John Wiley & Sons.

Benraiss-Noailles, L., & Viot, C. (2021). Employer brand equity effects on employees well-being and loyalty. *Journal of Business Research*, *126*, 605–613. https://doi.org/10.1016/j.jbusres.2020.02.002

Berthon, P., Ewing, M., & Hah, L. L. (2005). Captivating company: Dimensions of attractiveness in employer branding. *International Journal of Advertising*, *24*(2), 151–172. https://doi.org/10.1080/02650487.2005.11072912

Bretz, R. D. Jr, Ash, R. A., & Dreher, G. F. (1989). Do people make the place? An examination of the attraction-selection-attrition hypothesis. *Personnel Psychology*, *42*(3), 561–581. https://doi.org/10.1111/j.1744-6570.1989.tb00669.x

Cable, D. M., & Judge, T. A. (1994). Pay preferences and job search decisions: A person-organization fit perspective. *Personnel Psychology*, *47*(2), 317–348. https://doi.org/10.1111/j.1744-6570.1994.tb01727.x

Cable, D. M., & Turban, D. B. (2003). The value of organizational reputation in the recruitment context: A brand-equity perspective. *Journal of Applied Social Psychology*, *33*(11), 2244–2266. https://doi.org/10.1111/j.1559-1816.2003.tb01883.x

Cervellon, M. C., & Lirio, P. (2017). When employees don't "like" their employers on social media. *MIT Sloan Management Review*, *58*(2), 63–70.

Chatman, J. A. (1989). Improving interactional organizational research: A model of person-organization fit. *Academy of Management Review*, *14*(3), 333–349. https://doi.org/10.5465/amr.1989.4279063

Chatman, J. A. (1991). Matching people and organizations: Selection and socialization in public accounting firms. *Administrative Science Quarterly*, *36*(3), 459–484. https://doi.org/10.5465/ambpp.1989.4980837

Chinsky Matuson, R. (2013). *Talent magnetism: How to build a workplace that attracts and keeps the Best*. Nicholas Brealey Publishing.

Chun, R., & Davies, G. (2006). The influence of corporate character on customers and employees: Exploring similarities and differences. *Journal of the Academy of Marketing Science*, *34*(2), 138–146. https://doi.org/10.1177/0092070305284975

Davies, G. (2008). Employer branding and its influence on managers. *European Journal of Marketing*, *42*(5/6), 667–681. https://doi.org/10.1108/03090560810862570

Davies, G., & Chun, R. (2002). Gaps between the internal and external perceptions of the corporate brand. *Corporate Reputation Review*, *5*(2), 144–158. https://doi.org/10.1057/palgrave.crr.1540171

Davies, G., Chun, R., da Silva, R. V., & Roper, S. (2004). A corporate character scale to assess employee and customer views of organization reputation. *Corporate Reputation Review*, *7*(2), 125–146. https://doi.org/10.1057/palgrave.crr.1540216

Davies, G., Mete, M., & Whelan, S. (2018). When employer brand image aids employee satisfaction and engagement. *Journal of Organizational Effectiveness: People and Performance*, *5*(1), 64–80. https://doi.org/10.1108/JOEPP-03-2017-0028

Davis, S. M. (2000). The power of the brand. *Strategy & Leadership*, *28*(4), 49. https://doi.org/10.1108/10878570010378636

Elving, W. J., Westhoff, J. J., Meeusen, K., & Schoonderbeek, J. W. (2013). The war for talent? The relevance of employer branding in job advertisements for becoming an employer of choice. *Journal of Brand Management*, *20*(5), 355–373. https://doi.org/10.1057/bm.2012.21

Foster, C., Punjaisri, K., & Cheng, R. (2010). Exploring the relationship between corporate, internal and employer branding. *Journal of Product & Brand Management*, *19*(6), 401–409. https://doi.org/10.1108/10610421011085712

Gardner, B. B., & Levy, S. J. (1955). The product and the brand. *Harvard Business Review*, March–April, 33–39.

Gioia, D. A., Schultz, M., & Corley, K. G. (2000). Organizational identity, image, and adaptive instability. *Academy of Management Review*, *25*(1), 63–81. https://doi.org/10.5465/amr.2000.2791603

Heilmann, P., Saarenketo, S., & Liikkanen, K. (2013). Employer branding in power industry. *International Journal of Energy Sector Management*, *7*(2), 283–302. https://doi.org/10.1108/IJESM-03-2012-0003

Highhouse, S., Lievens, F., & Sinar, E. F. (2003). Measuring attraction to organizations. *Educational and Psychological Measurement*, *63*(6), 986–1001. https://doi.org/10.1177/0013164403258403

Iaffaldano, M. T., & Muchinsky, P. M. (1985). Job satisfaction and job performance: A meta-analysis. *Psychological Bulletin*, *97*(2), 251–273. https://doi.org/10.1037/0033-2909.97.2.251

Keeling, K. A., McGoldrick, P. J., & Sadhu, H. (2013). Staff word-of-mouth (SWOM) and retail employee recruitment. *Journal of Retailing*, *89*(1), 88–104. https://doi.org/10.1016/j.jretai.2012.11.003

Keller, K. L. (1993). Conceptualizing, measuring, and managing customer-based brand equity. *Journal of Marketing*, *57*(1), 1–22. https://doi.org/10.1177/002224299305700101

Keller, S., & Meaney, M. (2017). *Attracting and retaining the right talent*. McKinsey&Company.

Kotler, P. (1997). *Marketing management: Analysis, planning, implementation, and control* (9th ed.). Prentice-Hall.

Levitt, T. (1980). Marketing success through differentiation – Of anything. *Harvard Business Review*, *58*, 89–91.

Lievens, F., & Highhouse, S. (2003). The relation of instrumental and symbolic attributes to a company's attractiveness as an employer. *Personnel Psychology*, *56*(1), 75–102. https://doi.org/10.1111/j.1744-6570.2003.tb00144.x

Lievens, F., & Slaughter, J. E. (2016). Employer image and employer branding: What we know and what we need to know. *Annual Review of Organizational Psychology and Organizational Behavior*, *3*, 407–440. https://doi.org/10.1146/annurev-orgpsych-041015-062501

Logan, G. M. (1984). Loyalty and a sense of purpose. *California Management Review*, *27*(1), 149–156. https://doi.org/10.2307/41165119

Love, L. F., & Singh, P. (2011). Workplace branding: Leveraging human resources management practices for competitive advantage through "Best Employer" surveys. *Journal of Business and Psychology*, *26*(2), 175–181. https://doi.org/10.1007/s10869-011-9226-5

Men, L. R. (2014). Strategic internal communication: Transformational leadership, communication channels, and employee satisfaction. *Management Communication Quarterly*, *28*(2), 264–284. https://doi.org/10.1177/0893318914524536

Men, L. R., & Sung, Y. (2019). Shaping corporate character through symmetrical communication: The effects on employee-organization relationships. *International Journal of Business Communication*, 2329488418824989. https://doi.org/10.1177/2329488418824989

Men, L. R., & Tsai, W. H. S. (2015). Infusing social media with humanity: Corporate character, public engagement, and relational outcomes. *Public Relations Review*, *41*(3), 395–403. https://doi.org/10.1016/j.pubrev.2015.02.005

Miles, S. J., & Mangold, G. (2004). A conceptualization of the employee branding process. *Journal of Relationship Marketing*, *3*(2–3), 65–87. https://doi.org/10.1300/J366v03n02_05

Moroko, L., & Uncles, M. D. (2008). Characteristics of successful employer brands. *Journal of Brand Management*, *16*(3), 160–175. https://doi.org/10.1057/bm.2008.4

Morrison, E. W. (1996). Organizational citizenship behavior as a critical link between HRM practices and service quality. *Human Resource Management*, *35*(4), 493–512. https://doi.org/10.1002/(SICI)1099-050X(199624)35:4<493::AID-HRM4>3.0.CO;2-R

Pološki Vokić, N., Tkalac Verčič, A., & Sinčić Ćorić, D. (2021). *Strategic Internal Communication for Effective Internal Employer Branding* [Conference paper]. EUPRERA 2021 Congress, Pamplona, Spain.

Rampl, L. V. (2014). How to become an employer of choice: Transforming employer brand associations into employer first-choice brands. *Journal of Marketing Management*, *30*(13–14), 1486–1504. https://doi.org/10.1080/0267257X.2014.934903

Rampl, L. V., & Kenning, P. (2014). Employer brand trust and affect: Linking brand personality to employer brand attractiveness. *European Journal of Marketing*, *48*(1–2), 218–236. https://doi.org/10.1108/EJM-02-2012-0113

Rampl, L. V., Opitz, C., Welpe, I. M., & Kenning, P. (2016). The role of emotions in decision-making on employer brands: Insights from functional magnetic resonance imaging (fMRI). *Marketing Letters*, *27*(2), 361–374. https://doi.org/10.1007/s11002-014-9335-9

Rynes, S. L., & Barber, A. E. (1990). Applicant attraction strategies: An organizational perspective. *Academy of Management Review*, *15*(2), 286–310. https://doi.org/10.5465/amr.1990.4308158

Sartain, L., & Schumann, M. (2006). *Brand from the inside: Eight essentials to emotionally connect your employees to your business*. Jossey-Bass.

Schmit, M. J., & Allscheid, S. P. (1995). Employee attitudes and customer satisfaction: Making theoretical and empirical connections. *Personnel Psychology*, *48*(3), 521–536. https://doi.org/10.1111/j.1744-6570.1995.tb01768.x

Špoljarić, A., & Tkalac Verčič, A. (2022). Internal communication satisfaction and employee engagement as determinants of the employer brand. *Journal of Communication Management*, *26*(1), 130–148. https://doi.org/10.1108/JCOM-01-2021-0011

Terera, S. R., & Ngirande, H. (2014). The impact of rewards on job satisfaction and employee retention. *Mediterranean Journal of Social Sciences*, *5*(1), 481–487. https://doi.org/10.5901/mjss.2014.v5n1p481

Tkalac Verčič, A. (2021). The impact of employee engagement, organisational support and employer branding on internal communication satisfaction. *Public Relations Review*, *47*(1), 102009. https://doi.org/10.1016/j.pubrev.2021.102009

Tkalac Verčič, A., & Sinčić Ćorić, D. (2018). The relationship between reputation, employer branding and corporate social responsibility. *Public Relations Review*, *44*(4), 444–452. https://doi.org/10.1016/j.pubrev.2018.06.005

Tkalac Verčič, A., & Verčič, D. (2007). Reputation as matching identities and images: Extending Davies and Chun's research on gaps between the internal and external perceptions of the corporate brand. *Journal of Marketing Communications*, *13*(4), 277–290. https://doi.org/10.1080/13527260701300151

Tkalac Verčič, A., Galić, Z., & Žnidar, K. (2021a). The relationship of internal communication satisfaction with employee engagement and employer attractiveness: Testing the joint mediating effect of the social exchange quality indicators [Advanced online publication]. *International Journal of Business Communication.* https://doi.org/10.1177/23294884211053839

Tkalac Verčič, A., Verčič, D., & Špoljarić, A. (2021b). *The Effect of Covid on Internal Communication Channel Preference* [Conference presentation]. BledCom 2021, Bled, Slovenia.

Turban, D. B., & Keon, T. L. (1993). Organizational attractiveness: An interactionist perspective. *Journal of Applied Psychology*, *78*(2), 184–193. https://doi.org/10.1037/0021-9010.78.2.184

9 Organizational support and the psychological contract

Social exchange theory laid the foundations for understanding relationships between employees and their employers (Coyle-Shapiro & Shore, 2007). This relationship, also called the employee-organization relationship (EOR), is often defined by employees' perceptions of their employer and their experiences working at the organization. Among the various components of the EOR, perceived organizational support and psychological contract fulfillment appear to be the most salient for defining it. These indicators illustrate employees' perception of how much their organization values their contribution, is concerned about their well-being, and fulfills the promises and obligations it offered to them as employees under the so-called employment offer (see Chapter 8). As Eisenberger et al. (1990) put it, "positive discretionary actions by the organization that benefited the employee would be taken as evidence that the organization cared about one's well-being and therefore could be counted on for subsequent rewards" (p. 51).

If employees judge the EOR positively, there can be various positive outcomes for organizations, which ultimately increases organizational performance (Shore et al., 2009). For this reason, ensuring positive attitudes toward, and perceptions of, the organization as an employer is a crucial task of internal public relations practitioners.

In this chapter we describe our efforts to explore how communication practices within organizations influence employer brand perceptions and EOR management.

Social exchange theory

Social exchange theory grew mostly out of the work of Homans, Blau, and Emerson (Cook & Rice, 2003). These authors theorized social exchanges in similar yet different ways. Nowadays social exchange theory is considered one of the "most influential conceptual paradigms for understanding workplace behavior" (Cropanzano & Mitchell, 2005, p. 874). Social exchange theory has proven effective for designing and interpreting studies

DOI: 10.4324/9781003200109-9

of trust, affect, and emotion (Cook & Rice, 2003), all of which define the EOR (Shore et al., 2009).

Homans' theorization of social exchange

In 1958, Homans proposed that social behaviors form the foundation of a social exchange, which he defined in 1961 as "an exchange of activity, tangible or intangible, and more or less rewarding or costly, between at least two persons" (p. 13). While theorizing social exchange, Homans (1958) proposed the concept of equilibrium in social behaviors: there should be a balance between exchanging parties. This is consistent with Gouldner's (1960) norm of reciprocity, "a generalized moral norm … which defines certain actions and obligations as repayments for benefits received" (p. 170). Homans (1958) explained that in an exchange, a person provides something at a certain cost and also receives a reward. Social exchanges reach an equilibrium because all parties attempt to maximize their reward and minimize their cost. Homans' work focused on the parties in an exchange as individuals or part of small groups, and on parties' behavior during the exchange (Cook & Rice, 2003).

In the 1974 revision of his work, Homans introduced five social exchange propositions (as cited in Cook & Rice, 2003; Kullberg, 1977): the *success* proposition suggests that rewarded exchanges will be repeated; the *stimulus* proposition, that a person is more likely to repeat exchanges that are more similar to previous exchanges that resulted in a reward; the *value* proposition, that a person is more likely to participate in an exchange if the result of that exchange is valuable to him or her; the *deprivation-satiation* proposition, that the value of a certain reward decreases if more rewards were recently received, and increases if fewer rewards were recently received; and the *aggression-approval* proposition, that the lack of a reward (when expected) angers the person.

Homans' perhaps most significant contribution was the analysis of dyadic exchanges at the sub-institutional level of social exchange (Cook & Rice, 2003).

Blau's theorization of social exchange

Not long after Homans, Blau (1964) extensively described social exchange and what it represents. He defined this term as "voluntary actions of individuals that are motivated by the returns they are expected to bring and typically do in fact bring from others" (p. 91). The main distinction between Homans' and Blau's social exchange approaches is the perspective of time (Heath, 1976 as cited in Cook & Rice, 2003): while Homans (1958, 1961) suggested that participants in social exchange reflect on the past to determine which behaviors brought the greatest rewards at the lowest costs and should therefore be repeated, Blau (1964) suggested that participants *predict* which behavior will be most beneficial, i.e., they "anticipate rewards that benefit them" (p. 55).

Blau's (1964) work focused on larger groups than Homans' (1961), extending the concept of social exchange to organizations and the EOR. Nevertheless, Blau continued to examine the EOR from individual perspectives, and as a result, his work is referred to as micro-exchange theory. Blau was also concerned with power distribution and inequality in social exchanges. Such inequality can arise when some participants in the exchange possess more valuable resources than other participants, giving them power over the other participants.

Emerson's theorization of social exchange

From the early 1970s, Emerson undertook two lines of research, one that built on Homans' and Blau's theories by studying social exchange at the individual level (Cook & Rice, 2003), and another that scaled up social exchange theory to larger networks, creating the foundation for macro-exchange theory (Molm, 1994).

Forming the EOR

By helping to explain the EOR (Shore et al., 2009; Shore et al., 2004), social exchange theory can contribute greatly to the understanding of workplace behavior (Cropanzano & Mitchell, 2005). EORs comprise social exchanges, which are positive behaviors motivated by implicit expectations; and economic exchanges, which are based on formal contracts (Aryee et al., 2002; Shore et al., 2009). As Rhoades and Eisenberger (2002) concluded, employment is a "trade of effort and loyalty for tangible benefits and social rewards" (p. 698). Consistent with the premise of social exchange theory, favorable organizational behavior results in favorable employee behavior, including more positive attitudes and higher performance (e.g., Gould-Williams & Davies, 2005; Rhoades & Eisenberger, 2002; Rousseau, 1995; Tkalac Verčič et al., 2021; Wang et al., 2003).

A crucial part of EORs is trust: the employee must trust that an organization will reciprocate the employee's positive behavior (Gould-Williams & Davies, 2005; Mayer et al., 1995). Trust generates numerous positive outcomes for an organization, impacting employees' attitudes and behavior (Dirks & Ferrin, 2001). At the same time, the risk that employers will not reciprocate makes employees vulnerable (Mayer et al., 1995; Whitener, 1997) and places employers in a position of power (Blau, 1964). Shore et al. (2006) found that employees' trust in their organizations is based on the quality and frequency of social exchanges. By participating in quality social exchanges that generate trust, employees and employers alike invest in the EOR.

Social exchange relationships within an organization, including EORs, can be assessed using various social exchange quality indicators

(Tkalac Verčič et al., 2021). Below we define the two indicators that we applied in the research project from which this book emerged: organizational support and the psychological contract.

Perceived organizational support

Robbins and Judge (2013) defined perceived organizational support (POS) as the "degree to which employees believe that the organization values their contributions and cares about their well-being" (p. 81). In other words, POS refers to an employee's perception of the organization's commitment to him or her (Eisenberger et al., 1986), based on "experience-based attribution concerning the benevolent and malevolent intent of the organization's policies, norms, procedures, and actions, as they affect employees" (Eisenberger et al., 2001, p. 42). This perception of an organization personifies and humanizes it, making it capable of displaying benevolence toward its employees (Rhoades & Eisenberger, 2002). This personification of an organization has also allowed the use of social exchange theory, originally developed to explain interpersonal relationships, for analyzing EORs (Eisenberger et al., 1997). POS affects an employee's emotional affective commitment or "bond" with the organization (Rhoades et al., 2001). Higher POS increases employees' feeling of duty to the organization (Eisenberger et al., 2001), which in turn strengthens their loyalty and dedication (Rhoades et al., 2001) and leads to "greater job-related efforts, resulting in enhanced in-role job performance and extrarole performance helpful to the organization" (Kurtessis et al., 2017, p. 1856).

The psychological contract

Employees and organizations have implicit expectations about each other (Cullinane & Dundon, 2006; Robinson & Morrison, 2000), which can be conceptualized as a psychological contract. This contract, which is unwritten, establishes the mutual expectations within EORs (Robbins & Judge, 2013). It constitutes "an exchange agreement between individuals and their organization" based on "beliefs … shaped by the organization" (Rousseau, 1995, p. 9) as well as on "external messages and social cues from the organization or the social setting and the individual's internal interpretations, predispositions, and constructions" (Rousseau, 1995, p. 34).

Employees evaluate whether the organization is fulfilling the psychological contract, based on their own and colleagues' experiences within the organization (Ho, 2005). Whether an employee perceives the psychological contract as fulfilled plays a crucial role in the EOR (Ho & Levesque, 2005): it affects his or her loyalty (Turnley & Feldman, 1999) and trust in the organization (Robinson, 1996). Social exchange theory (Blau, 1964) and the norm of reciprocity (Gouldner, 1960) lead to the hypothesis that, just as in the case of POS, an employer's fulfillment of employee expectations improves employee performance.

The unwritten nature of the psychological contract makes it subjective (Morrison & Robinson, 1997; Rousseau, 1989). This means that an employee's perception of whether the psychological contract is fulfilled can differ completely from the organization's perception (Coyle-Shapiro et al., 2019). In fact, most employees analyzed in studies of the psychological contract perceive that the organization has breached the contract (e.g., Conway & Briner, 2002; Robinson & Rousseau, 1994). Such a perception may well limit employees' job performance and therefore organizational performance overall.

Internal communication and employer branding in the context of social exchange theory

Internal communication is used to manage behavior, create feedback, share emotions, persuade, and exchange information in an organization (Robbins & Judge, 2013). Using communication to manage expectations and employee perceptions can have great positive outcomes for organizations (Špoljarić & Verčič, 2022). Internal communication needs to be clear and two-way to ensure that employees are satisfied with what they receive from the employer (Tkalac Verčič et al., 2021).

The sparse research on the relationship between internal communication and social exchange indicators suggests a significant connection between the two (Allen, 1992; Tkalac Verčič, 2021). Allen (1992) showed that some forms of communication strongly impact organizational commitment through POS. This finding is consistent with Blau's (1964) social exchange theory and theories about EORs (Dirks & Ferrin, 2001). We have shown that POS can predict ICS (Tkalac Verčič, 2021), which in turn can indirectly influence employee engagement and employer attractiveness via POS (Tkalac Verčič et al., 2021).

Even sparser than research analyzing internal communication and POS is research analyzing communication and psychological contract fulfillment. The latter type of analysis is particularly important given that such fulfillment involves expectations and perceptions, which arise through communication and are influenced by it (Clutterbuck, 2005). Psychological contract fulfillment is significantly related to job communication (Guest & Conway, 2002), and it mediates the relationships of ICS with employee engagement and employer attractiveness (Tkalac Verčič et al., 2021).

Internal communication can manage expectations and perceptions of employer brand (Backhaus & Tikoo, 2004; Ruchika & Prasad, 2017), but we are aware of very few studies analyzing the relationships of employer brand with organizational support or psychological contract fulfillment.

Affective commitment, which is an emotional bond that an employee has with the organization, reflects the organization's contribution to personal development, which is a part of the development value of employer attractiveness. Commitment is positively related with POS (Eisenberger et al., 2001; Meyer & Allen, 1991; Rhoades et al., 2001), as well as with employee attractiveness, perception of job security, and psychological contract fulfillment (Hendry & Jenkins, 1997). More recent work has suggested that the skills attained at a job, which are a part of the development value of employer attractiveness, influence a perception of psychological contract fulfillment (Baruch, 2004), and therefore presumably employer attractiveness. We are aware of only one study that has analyzed employer attractiveness as an antecedent of employer brand, and as a factor connected to psychological contract fulfillment (Tkalac Verčič et al., 2021).

We explored relationships of ICS dimensions with social exchange quality indicators (Table 9.1) and employer attractiveness (Table 9.2). All correlations were significant and either moderate ($.36 < r < .67$) or strong ($.68 < r < .90$), based on the cutoff of Taylor (1990).

We found that ICS correlated strongly with psychological contract fulfillment and POS. These strong correlations were expected in light of previous studies (e.g., Allen, 1992; Clutterbuck, 2005; Guest & Conway, 2002; Tkalac Verčič, 2021; Tkalac Verčič et al., 2021).

Correlations of both psychological contract fulfillment and POS with employer attractiveness were found to be strong. The dimension of employer attractiveness called "development value" strongly correlated with psychological contract fulfillment and POS, consistent with previous studies (e.g., Eisenberger et al., 2001; Meyer & Allen, 1991; Rhoades et al., 2001). Another employer attractiveness dimension, "economic value", also correlated with psychological contract fulfillment and POS. These strong correlations were expected given that economic value reflects job security and expected opportunities, which are also part of psychological contract fulfillment. Economic value also reflects perception of opportunities and financial rewards that an organization ensures for its employees, which explains the strong correlation between POS and economic value. Interest value strongly correlated with POS, which is expected given that both constructs reflect the feeling of being valued by an employer.

Conclusion

The theory of social exchange, first developed mainly by Homans, Blau, and Emerson in the 1960s and 1970s, has created a paradigm for understanding EORs. This theory conceptualized communication between individuals, stipulating that people participate in behaviors that benefit them and result in benevolent behavior toward them. The theory led to

Table 9.1 Pearson correlation coefficients between ICS dimensions and social exchange quality indicators

		SwF	*SwIS*	*SwHC*	*SwIC*	*SwIO*	*SwCC*	*SwQM*	*SwCM*	*ICS*
PCF	Pearson correlation	.666	.627	.530	.589	.620	.656	.599	.625	.698
	Sig. (2-tailed)	.001***	.001***	.001***	.001***	.001***	.001***	.001***	.001***	.001***
POS	Pearson Correlation	.758	.657	.540	.625	.667	.730	.623	.661	.748
	Sig. (2-tailed)	.001***	.001***	.001***	.001***	.001***	.001***	.001***	.001***	.001***

Legend: ICS, internal communication satisfaction; SwCC, satisfaction with communication climate; SwCM, satisfaction with communication in meetings; SwF, satisfaction with feedback; SwHC, satisfaction with horizontal communication; SwIC, satisfaction with informal communication; SwIO, satisfaction with information about the organization; SwIS, satisfaction with communication with immediate superior; SwQM, satisfaction with the quality of communication media; PCF, psychological contract fulfillment; POS, perceived organizational support.

*** $p < .001$.

Table 9.2 Pearson correlation coefficients between dimensions of employer attractiveness and social exchange quality indicators

		IV	*SV*	*EV*	*DV*	*AV*	*EA*
PCF	Pearson correlation	.664	.564	.698	.689	.657	.713
	Sig. (2-tailed)	.001***	.001***	.001***	.001***	.001***	.001***
POS	Pearson Correlation	.717	.615	.725	.746	.700	.763
	Sig. (2-tailed)	.001***	.001***	.001***	.001***	.001***	.001***

Legend: AV, application value; DV, development value; EV, economic value; EA, employer attractiveness; IV, interest value; SV, social value; PCF, psychological contract fulfillment; POS, perceived organizational support.

*** $p < .001$.

the idea that benevolent behavior by organizations will be reciprocated by their employees, generating positive organizational outcomes. However, the theory of social exchange has rarely been used to analyze internal communication and employer branding, both of which are key to EORs.

Social exchange quality indicators, in particular POS and psychological contract fulfillment, can be used to measure satisfaction with EORs. POS measures how much an employee feels valued and cared for by the organization, while psychological contract fulfillment measures to what extent an organization fulfills an employee's implicit expectations. Both measures can be managed and increased through internal communication, in turn improving employees' perception of the employer brand.

References

Allen, M. W. (1992). Communication and organizational commitment: Perceived organizational support as a mediating factor. *Communication Quarterly*, *40*(4), 357–367. https://doi.org/10.1080/01463379209369852

Aryee, S., Budhwar, P. S., & Chen, Z. X. (2002). Trust as a mediator of the relationship between organizational justice and work outcomes: Test of a social exchange model. *Journal of Organizational Behavior*, *23*(3), 267–285. https://doi.org/10.1002/job.138

Backhaus, K., & Tikoo, S. (2004). Conceptualizing and researching employer branding. *Career Development International*, *9*(5), 501–517. https://doi.org/10.1108/13620430410550754

Baruch, Y. (2004). *Managing careers: Theory and practice*. Pearson Education.

Blau, P. M. (1964). *Exchange and power in social life*. Wiley.

Clutterbuck, D. (2005). Communication and the psychological contract. *Journal of Communication Management*, *9*(4), 359–364. https://doi.org/10.1108/13632540510621597

Conway, N., & Briner, R. B. (2002). A daily diary study of affective responses to psychological contract breach and exceeded promises. *Journal of Organizational Behavior*, *23*(3), 287–302. https://doi.org/10.1002/job.139

Cook, K. S., & Rice, E. (2003). Social exchange theory. In J. Delamater (Ed.), *Handbook of social psychology* (pp. 53–76). Kluwer Academic/Plenum Publishers.

Coyle-Shapiro, J. A. M., Pereira Costa, S., Doden, W., & Chang, C. (2019). Psychological contracts: Past, present, and future. *Annual Review of Organizational Psychology and Organizational Behavior*, *6*, 145–169. https://doi.org/10.1146/annurev-orgpsych-012218-015212

Coyle-Shapiro, J. A., & Shore, L. M. (2007). The employee–organization relationship: Where do we go from here? *Human resource Management Review*, *17*(2), 166–179. https://doi.org/10.1016/j.hrmr.2007.03.008

Cropanzano, R., & Mitchell, M. S. (2005). Social exchange theory: An interdisciplinary review. *Journal of Management*, *31*(6), 874–900. https://doi.org/10.1177/0149206305279602

Cullinane, N., & Dundon, T. (2006). The psychological contract: A critical review. *International Journal of Management Reviews*, *8*(2), 113–129. https://doi.org/10.1111/j.1468-2370.2006.00123.x

Dirks, K. T., & Ferrin, D. L. (2001). The role of trust in organizational settings. *Organization Science*, *12*(4), 450–467. https://doi.org/10.1287/orsc.12.4.450.10640

Eisenberger, R., Armeli, S., Rexwinkel, B., Lynch, P. D., & Rhoades, L. (2001). Reciprocation of perceived organizational support. *Journal of Applied Psychology*, *86*(1), 42–51. https://doi.org/10.1037/0021-9010.86.1.42

Eisenberger, R., Cummings, J., Armeli, S., & Lynch, P. (1997). Perceived organizational support, discretionary treatment, and job satisfaction. *Journal of Applied Psychology*, *82*(5), 812–820. https://doi.org/10.1037/0021-9010.82.5.812

Eisenberger, R., Fasolo, P., & Davis-LaMastro, V. (1990). Perceived organizational support and employee diligence, commitment, and innovation. *Journal of Applied Psychology*, *75*(1), 51. https://doi.org/10.1037/0021-9010.75.1.51

Eisenberger, R., Huntington, R., Hutchison, S., & Sowa, D. (1986). Perceived organizational support. *Journal of Applied Psychology*, *71*(3), 500–507. https://doi.org/10.1037/0021-9010.71.3.500

Gouldner, A. W. (1960). The norm of reciprocity: A preliminary statement. *American Sociological Review*, *25*(2), 161–178. https://doi.org/10.2307/2092623

Gould-Williams, J., & Davies, F. (2005). Using social exchange theory to predict the effects of HRM practice on employee outcomes: An analysis of public sector workers. *Public Management Review*, *7*(1), 1–24. https://doi.org/10.1080/1471903042000339392

Guest, D. E., & Conway, N. (2002). Communicating the psychological contract: An employer perspective. *Human resource Management Journal*, *12*(2), 22–38. https://doi.org/10.1111/j.1748-8583.2002.tb00062.x

Hendry, C., & Jenkins, R. (1997). Psychological contracts and new deals. *Human Resource Management Journal*, *7*(1), 38.

Ho, V. T. (2005). Social influence on evaluations of psychological contract fulfillment. *Academy of Management Review*, *30*(1), 113–128. https://doi.org/10.5465/amr.2005.15281438

Ho, V. T., & Levesque, L. L. (2005). With a little help from my friends (and substitutes): Social referents and influence in psychological contract fulfillment. *Organization Science*, *16*(3), 275–289. https://doi.org/10.1287/orsc.1050.0121

Homans, G. C. (1958). Social behavior as exchange. *American Journal of Sociology*, *63*(6), 597–606.

Homans, G. C. (1961). *Social behavior: Its elementary forms*. Harcourt, Brace & World, Inc.

Kullberg, V. K. (1977). Toward a formal statement of Homans' social exchange propositions. *Humboldt Journal of Social Relations*, *4*(2), 9–20.

Kurtessis, J. N., Eisenberger, R., Ford, M. T., Buffardi, L. C., Stewart, K. A., & Adis, C. S. (2017). Perceived organizational support: A meta-analytic evaluation of organizational support theory. *Journal of Management*, *43*(6), 1854–1884. https://doi.org/10.1177/0149206315575554

Mayer, R. C., Davis, J. H., & Schoorman, F. D. (1995). An integrative model of organizational trust. *Academy of Management Review*, *20*(3), 709–734. https://doi.org/10.5465/amr.1995.9508080335

Meyer, J. P., & Allen, N. J. (1991). A three-component conceptualization of organizational commitment. *Human resource Management Review*, *1*(1), 61–89. https://doi.org/10.1016/1053-4822(91)90011-Z

Molm, L. D. (1994). Dependence and risk: Transforming the structure of social exchange. *Social Psychology Quarterly*, *57*(3), 163–176. https://doi.org/10.2307/2786874

Morrison, E. W., & Robinson, S. L. (1997). When employees feel betrayed: A model of how psychological contract violation develops. *Academy of management Review*, *22*(1), 226–256. https://doi.org/10.5465/amr.1997.9707180265.

Rhoades, L., & Eisenberger, R. (2002). Perceived organizational support: A review of the literature. *Journal of Applied Psychology*, *87*(4), 698–714. https://doi.org/10.1037//0021-9010.87.4.698

Rhoades, L., Eisenberger, R., & Armeli, S. (2001). Affective commitment to the organization: The contribution of perceived organizational support. *Journal of Applied Psychology*, *86*(5), 825–836. https://doi.org/10.1037/0021-9010.86.5.825

Robbins, S. P., & Judge, T. A. (2013). *Organizational behavior* (18th ed.). Pearson Education.

Robinson, S. L. (1996). Trust and breach of the psychological contract. *Administrative Science Quarterly*, *41*(4), 574–599. https://doi.org/10.2307/2393868

Robinson, S. L., & Morrison, E. W. (2000). The development of psychological contract breach and violation: A longitudinal study. *Journal of Organizational Behavior*, *21*(5), 525–546. https://doi.org/10.1002/1099-1379(200008)21:5<525::AID-JOB40>3.0.CO;2-T

Robinson, S. L., & Rousseau, D. M. (1994). Violating the psychological contract: Not the exception but the norm. *Journal of Organizational Behavior*, *15*(3), 245–259. https://doi.org/10.1002/job.4030150306

Rousseau, D. M. (1989). Psychological and implied contracts in organizations. *Employee responsibilities and rights journal*, *2*(2), 121–139. https://doi.org/10.1007/BF01384942

Rousseau, D. M. (1995). *Psychological contracts in organisations: Understanding written and unwritten agreements*. Sage Publications.

Ruchika, & Prasad, A. (2017). Untapped relationship between employer branding, anticipatory psychological contract and intent to join. *Global Business Review*, *20*(1), 194–213. https://doi.org/10.1177/0972150917713897

Shore, L. M., Tetrick, L. E., Lynch, P., & Barksdale, K. (2006). Social and economic exchange: Construct development and validation. *Journal of Applied Social Psychology*, *36*(4), 837–867. https://doi.org/10.1111/j.0021-9029.2006.00046.x

Shore, L. M., Tetrick, L. E., Taylor, M. S., Jaqueline, A. M., Liden, R. C., Parks, J. M., & Van Dyne, L. (2004). The employee-organization relationship: A timely concept in a period of transition. In J. Martocchio (Ed.), *Research in personnel and human resources management* (Vol. 23, pp. 291–370). Emerald Publishing. https://doi.org/10.1016/S0742-7301(04)23007-9

Shore, L. M., Bommer, W. H., Rao, A. N., & Seo, J. (2009). Social and economic exchange in the employee-organization relationship: The moderating role of reciprocation wariness. *Journal of Managerial Psychology*, *24*(8), 701–721. https://doi.org/10.1108/02683940910996752

Špoljarić, A., & Verčič, D. (2022). *The effects of social exchange quality indicators on employee engagement through internal communication* [Manuscript submitted for publication]. Faculty of Economics & Business Zagreb, University of Zagreb.

Taylor, R. (1990). Interpretation of the correlation coefficient: A basic review. *Journal of Diagnostic Medical Sonography*, *6*(1), 35–39. https://doi.org/10.1177/875647939000600106

Tkalac Verčič, A. (2021). The impact of employee engagement, organisational support and employer branding on internal communication satisfaction. *Public Relations Review*, *47*(1), 102009. https://doi.org/10.1016/j.pubrev.2021.102009

Tkalac Verčič, A., Galić, Z., & Žnidar, K. (2021). The relationship of internal communication satisfaction with employee engagement and employer attractiveness: Testing the joint mediating effect of the social exchange quality indicators [Advanced online publication]. *International Journal of Business Communication*. https://doi.org/10.1177/23294884211053839

Turnley, W. H., & Feldman, D. C. (1999). The impact of psychological contract violations on exit, voice, loyalty, and neglect. *Human Relations*, *52*(7), 895–922. https://doi.org/10.1177/001872679905200703

Wang, D., Tsui, A. S., Zhang, Y., & Ma, L. (2003). Employment relationships and firm performance: Evidence from an emerging economy. *Journal of Organizational Behavior*, *24*(5), 511–535. https://doi.org/10.1002/job.213

Whitener, E. M. (1997). The impact of human resource activities on employee trust. *Human Resource Management Review*, *7*(4), 389–404. https://doi.org/10.1016/S1053-4822(97)90026-7

10 A model of internal communication

The practical implications of our research can be summed up in a model of internal communication that consists of four components. First, there is a strategic management function: running a business means developing and nurturing sense of purpose and daily communication among associates and employees. Second, there is an essential managerial function: managing people means communicating with them. Third, internal communication fulfills a specialized function – based on expertise – of envisioning, organizing, executing, and assessing the role of communication in constituting and driving the organization and its success. Fourth, internal communication fulfills the function of enabling members of an organization to achieve communication competence.

A model of internal communication

In the research project from which this book emerged, we have explored what is internal communication, how it is positioned in contemporary organizations, how it can be strategized, which channels it uses, and how it can be evaluated. We have also examined how satisfaction with internal communication affects perceived organizational support and perceived psychological agreement, which then act as intervening variables that influence employer engagement and employer branding. Now, can this knowledge be applied to the practice of internal communication? We are strong believers in Lewin's (1943) dictum that "There is nothing more practical than a good theory" (p. 118). In the present chapter, we re-conceptualize internal communication into a model that can help organizations make informed decisions and select where to intervene in order to upgrade their practices.

Nearly a century has passed since Barnard (1938/1956), in one of the first and most influential books on management, *The Function of the Executive*, noted that authority is a function of communication. If a manager wants to guide and motivate an employee, there must be communication between them. Communication constitutes organizations (Schoenenborn et al., 2019) and can therefore be considered a generic function of every

DOI: 10.4324/9781003200109-10

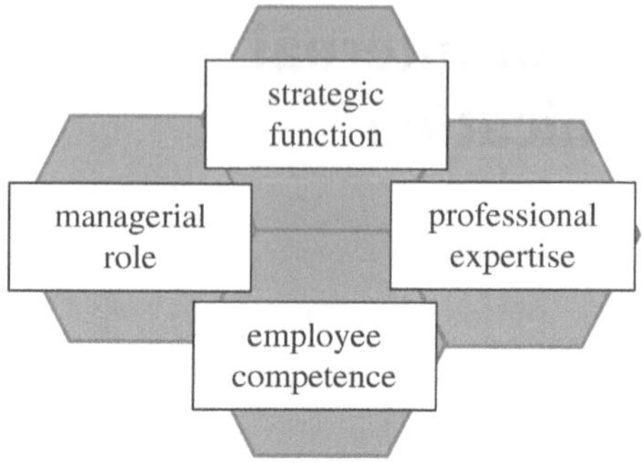

Figure 10.1 Four-component model of internal communication.

organization. If we want to improve the quality of internal communication in order to influence the attitudes that employees hold toward an organization, what elements of internal communication should we consider?

The model in Figure 10.1 deconstructs the process that we have studied using the research model in Chapter 1. We have shown in Chapter 2 that internal communication is becoming a separate, specialized function based on specific *expertise* that deals with the process of internal communication, its antecedents and consequents, use of communication media, and evaluation of success. In Chapter 3 we have shown how internal communication must be treated as a strategic management *function* responsible for the overall mission and vision of internal communication in organizations, preferably capable of supporting dynamic strategizing by management, who can thereby adjust "on the fly" as circumstances change. Our interviewees informed us that the role of managers as communicators is essential, yet often overlooked. Although communication experts can perform some of the functions that managers should take on for themselves, it is essential that managers understand that internal communication is an important managerial *role* and that there is no good manager without good communication. Finally, exploiting the full potential of all members of organizations requires active cooperation and alignment between management and employees, which in turn requires that members possess the necessary communication competence within an organizational context. These considerations are increasingly important as organizations focus on services, and as knowledge workers dominate the workforce.

The model of internal communication in Figure 10.1 is a holistic one that follows Kalla's suggestion to view internal communication as *integrated*, in other words as "all formal and informal communication taking place internally at all levels of an organization" (2005, p. 304). At the same time, the model takes into account that internal communication is not something that "just happens" in organizations. It has a specific function of guiding and steering organizational processes; it is "the strategic management of interactions and relationships between stakeholders within organizations" (Welch & Jackson, 2007, p. 184). As organizations grow and become more complex, specialist knowledge and expertise become increasingly important for managing and executing key purposeful interventions in internal communication structures, processes, and actions. Our model also recognizes that for understanding and managing internal communication as relational processes among management, among employees, and between management and employees, employees must be recognized as active participants in the processes. In this way, successful internal communication contains not only components of strategic function, managerial role, and functional expertise, but it also depends on communication competence from the lowest to highest levels of the organization. This model aims to support our definition of internal communication proposed in Chapter 1: internal communication is the management of communication between an organization and its members in order to inform, motivate, engage, and co-create meaning with the purpose of making organizations more effective.

Heide et al. (2018) presented a similar view of communication in organizations, the goal of which is what they term the "communicative organization". Based on research conducted between 2014 and 2018 by researchers at the Institution for Strategic Communication at Lund University in Sweden, Heide et al. (2018) defined the communicative organization as follows:

> A communicative organization has constant communication on its agenda. It is widely understood within the organization that communication is a prerequisite for an organization's existence, goal fulfillment, and success. Having a well thought-out, well-functioning communication system is fundamental. Within the communicative organization different voices are valued and actively listened to; this allows the organization to develop, adapt to changes, and be a leader in its field. Dialogue is valued as a means of achieving sufficient mutual understanding to be able to act in a tactful way. Managers and employees have communicative skills and take responsibility for communication. The organizational culture is in line with the organization's business objective and supports the employees in their communicative tasks. The communication professionals are communication experts and drive the organization's communicative development.
>
> (p. 9)

The above definition of the communicative organizations is a normative ideal of how organizations should successfully conduct internal communication. This definition contains all four elements of our model of internal communication: internal communication is a strategic function ("communication is a prerequisite for an organization's existence, goal fulfillment, and success"), a managerial role ("[m]anagers ... have communicative skills and take responsibility for communication"), a functional specialization ("communication professionals are communication experts and drive the organization's communicative development), and communication competence of all employees ("employees have communicative skills and take responsibility for communication").

We believe that our model of internal communication provides a heuristic tool for further exploration of internal communication in contemporary organizations.

Internal communication as a strategic management function

Founding an organization and helping it grow and develop mean communicating with and taking care of people in order to organize work and relationships within an organization, as well as between the organization and its environment. In this sense, communication is a central concept in management (Thompkins, 1987). Entrepreneurs and managers must be able to share their views and visions with others in order to guide and motivate them to produce results. In this way, internal communication means strategic use of communication in organizations. When organizational leaders contemplate how to structure work processes and perform activities, they are contemplating about communication processes. By stipulating who is responsible for whom, who works with whom and who reports to whom, the leaders are structuring communication.

Internal communication influences organizational outcomes and top management is responsible for its strategic use. As we have demonstrated in our research project, communication satisfaction affects perceived psychological contract fulfillment and perceived organizational support, which serve as intervening variables influencing employee engagement and employer brand; these last two factors are crucial intangible assets in every organization. Creation and protection of material and immaterial assets is the ultimate responsibility of business management, and by contributing to wealth creation, internal communication serves a strategic management function, i.e., "strategic internal communication" (Men, 2021). This should be the ultimate responsibility of the CEO, or at least one member of the Board.

In the first issue of the *International Journal of Strategic Communication* in 2007, the term strategic communication was defined as "the purposeful use of communication by an organization to fulfill its mission" (Hallahan et al., 2007, p. 3). This definition was updated 10 years later (Zerfass et al., 2018, p. 493): "Strategic communication encompasses all communication that is substantial for the survival and sustained success of an entity. Specifically, strategic communication is the purposeful use of communication by an organization or other entity to engage in conversations of strategic significance to its goals". Strategic communication covers both internal and external communication, but sometimes the former is overshadowed by the latter in integrated corporate communication departments that are more concerned with the organization's relationship to its external environment than with what happens within the organization. This is one of the reasons why internal communication has evolved into an independent department focused on communication within the organization.

Before internal communication materializes in messages and media, it must be codified in organizational design and policies, which can occur even when decision-makers do not fully understand the implications of the internal communication policy or strategy. Thus, somebody at the highest levels of management should understand the implications of visions, plans, and decisions for internal communication. As we have pointed out, "Managers are the ones who are responsible for the communication policies of an organization and the way in which (members of) an organization communicate" (Ruler & Verčič, 2005, p. 241). This holds even when organizations do not consciously consider the implications of management decisions on internal communication.

If an organization today wants to be good or even excellent, it must understand the role of communication in its constitution and growth, which means that its leadership should assume responsibility for understanding and managing internal communication as one of the most important business processes. Some organizations that we studied in our research project understood that, and they held top management directly responsible for internal communication.

Internal communication as a managerial role

In his seminal study on *The Nature of Managerial Work*, Mintzberg (1973) found that managers spent two thirds of their time communicating, which led him to describe the manager as an information processing center. Managers serve as the nerve centers of organizations. They monitor external information in their role as liaisons, collecting information from their contacts, informers, peers, and experts. They monitor internal information in their role as leaders, collecting information from their subordinates. Because of their access to critical information, managers can disseminate information to subordinates and serve as spokespeople delivering information to outsiders and as strategy-makers who identify problems and opportunities.

Management is much more than planning, organizing, executing, and measuring how work is done. It also means informing, educating, and motivating employees, as well as helping them find meaning in what they do. It is not surprising that professional communication specialists think their most important responsibility in the future will be to train managers to act as communicators (Zerfass et al., 2009). This communicative role of managers is generally known as *managerial communication* (Veltsos & Hynes, 2022).

Managerial communication can be taught as a set of skills for conveying messages through speaking, writing, and using contemporary digital technology. But managerial communication is much more. Managers must understand factors that affect communication, which can include culture, ethnicity, sexual orientation and gender identity, disabilities, age, generational differences, and education (Veltsos & Hynes, 2022).

Managers must understand that communication is more than moving information from point A to point B. Communication is a performative process (Gulbrandsen & Just, 2020): a manager's presentation and visibility – or his or her absence – speaks volumes. Words, images, and sounds have tangible consequences: managers can improve, repair, or harm relationships in organizations. Research has repeatedly confirmed that quality of communication with superiors is among the strongest predictors of overall employee satisfaction with communication in an organization.

For managerial communication to be successful, managers must know and understand their responsibility for communicating and for ensuring the satisfaction of their employees, colleagues, and superiors with that communication. Managers must train in order to improve their communication knowledge and skills. They must understand how contingency factors and competitive pressures affect communication processes, and they must appreciate the ethical dilemmas that managers, as people in a position of power, face when communicating with others, particularly their subordinates (Veltsos & Hynes, 2022).

Managers require appropriate knowledge, skills, and attitudes, as well as capacities and tools in order to conduct good internal communication. Communicating with people takes time, and managerial positions should be structured to ensure adequate time for this human element. In addition to time, good communication requires money, e.g., to ensure the availability and skilled use of communication tools such as audiovisual presentations and computer-assisted techniques. Life-long education in managerial communication, including internal communication, is becoming a necessity for ensuring highly qualified and motivated managerial capital in an organization.

The development of competencies in managerial internal communication should be remunerated appropriately: promotion schemes should signal to managers that internal communication is an important role that they must play. Managers should understand that their income and career depend on their business results in the short and long term, and on how well they nurture the human capital entrusted to them.

Throughout this book we have considered internal communication as intrinsically linked to what managers do: they conduct such communication constantly, even if they do not do so in a conscious or premeditated manner. Internal communication is an important role for managers, and they should understand that and develop their competence in managerial communication accordingly. The strategic function of internal communication gives value to managerial communication and can turn it into an important competitive advantage of the organization.

Internal communication as an expertise

At the turn of the 20th century, production of internal messaging and media began to emerge as the expertise of internal communication. The first internal communication specialists were in-house "industrial" journalists, who were later joined by public relations or corporate communication specialists. These experts were concerned primarily with external audiences, but they also helped top managers create messages for internal publics. As organizations grew and became more complex, the dedicated profession of internal communication specialist emerged, followed by the appearance of entire internal communication departments.

There is a long line of research into what communication specialists do and how they fulfill their roles (Broom & Smith, 1979). The most important roles in public relations and communication management are communication manager and communication technician (Dozier & Broom, 1995). Communication technicians perform many activities, from writing, designing, and circulating newsletters to designing websites and organizing events. These technicians may be highly qualified writers, designers, and photographers, but they implement what they are told in order to produce tools used in communication. Communication managers, in contrast, are responsible for conceptualizing communication processes, budgeting, planning, organizing, evaluating, and generally managing communication. The distinction between technicians and managers in internal communication is similar to that in other professions, such as between nurses and physicians in the health sector. Nurses and technicians are extremely important and probably do the majority of work, but managers and physicians are educated and trained to develop strategies and implement them.

Recent research has extended our understanding of the roles played by professionals in public relations and communication management. Zerfass et al. (2021) distinguish five roles that communication specialists perform, often simultaneously, during their workday: Advisor, Ambassador, Coach, Communicator, and Manager. The most frequent role is the Communicator, who creates campaigns and content as well as manages media, among other things; followed by the Manager, who hires and fires people, defines processes and structures, as well as allocates budgets, among other things; and then the Coach, who provides content for speeches, presentations, and social media posts, as well as offers communication training; and finally the Advisor, who interprets trends in society and explains the corresponding opportunities and risks for internal stakeholder expectations. The least frequent role is Ambassador, who is responsible for communicating corporate strategies internally and for personally convincing important decision-makers and influencers.

In his study of internal communication in large companies in Europe, Nelli (2018) found that 36% of internal communication departments reported to corporate communication departments, 22% directly to CEOs and 19% to human relations departments. Similarly, our study of mid-size corporations in Croatia showed that internal communication managers reported to corporate communications managers, human resources managers, or directly to CEOs. These findings are in line with previous reports that internal communication is located mostly in communication departments (Helsby, 2002). However, in their study in Latvia, Zaumane and Leščevica (2021) found functional responsibility for internal communication management to be part of public relations (corporate communication), human resources, and marketing.

The size and geographic spread of an organization are the best predictors of whether internal communication is differentiated from other communication functions within that organization, whether specialized experts in internal communication have emerged in that organization, and whether the organization has an independent internal communication department (Nelli, 2018). As companies grow in size and geographic spread, their internal complexity increases and creates greater need for appropriate experts. For example, as contemporary organizations become larger and/or more fluid, there is greater need for professionals who can help manage and adapt to organizational change and transformation.

Fifteen years of research on the communication profession in Europe led Tench et al. (2017) to propose that excellent communication professionals in Europe must be *sagacious* (knowledgeable, with reflective wisdom and good judgment), *linked* (with people, media, and networks), and *solid* (strong, sensitive, and savvy). They should also understand "that *conflicts of interest* are a fundamental part of living together as humans and therefore also of organizational life" (Tench et al., 2017, p. 187). This highlights the importance of ethics in internal communication and raises the question, "How are internal communication experts equipped to deal with it?"

Internal communication as communication competence

Humans communicate differently within organizations than outside them. Within organizations, communication is affected by many factors that can make it differ from communication in private or social life. For example, someone who is a dictatorial boss at work can be a submissive partner at home, and *vice versa*. Knowing how to behave and communicate at work is essential for all employees. While strategic (corporate) internal communication build and nurture the intangible internal assets of organizations (engagement and employer brand), communication between employees at the same level (peer communication) makes collaborative work possible and is the primary task in a service economy. This was already apparent before the turn of the century, when Cooper and Jackson (1997) noted in a handbook for future research on organizational behavior that as organizations become flexible, so too will employees, who will become more communicative in the process.

In their stakeholder approach to internal communication, Welch and Jackson (2007) identified four types of internal communication involving different internal stakeholders: internal line manager communication, internal team peer communication, internal project peer communication, and internal corporate communication. Only internal corporate communication is concerned with how top management communicates with all employees of an organization, which can occur as one-way, top-down interaction in which one side (management) actively produces communication and the other side (employees) passively consumes it. Even in this scenario, however, communication cannot succeed unless the recipients are able and willing to receive the messages sent to them. In this way, every organization demands a minimum of competence in organizational communication from its employees. Such competence means mastery of the organizational language, skills in listening and reading and, for an increasing proportion of employees, digital skills.

The minimal communication competence required of employees is different for the same position at different organizations as well as for different positions within the same organization. Some manual industrial jobs demand less communication competence than jobs in services, while knowledge-intensive and collaborative jobs demand higher levels of communication competence, such as a team of 10–20 medical specialists, doctors, nurses, and technicians performing surgery during 24 hours, or an agency sending a manned mission into space. Communicating as a line manager or within collaborative teams requires communication competencies beyond the minimal level. Thus, managing internal communication means managing communication needs and competencies of employees at different levels in the organization. As Men and Bowen note, "Internal communication is the strategic management of internal communication in managing interdependence and building mutually beneficial relationships between the organization and its employees" (2017, p. 12). Mutuality in relationships presupposes mutual activity of both parties, and indeed internal communication, however strategically directed by management, depends equally on management and employees. Successful internal communication is therefore a function of the communication competence of all members of the organization.

At the same time, internal communication competence is not equal across all members of an organization, and it should increase with the number of people for whom a manager is responsible: managing five people demands greater competence than managing 50, 500, 500, or 50,000 people. Vertical promotion in a career should involve an increase in communication competence, which is critical for meeting the challenges of increasing cultural, ethnic, and sexual diversity in contemporary organizations.

We hypothesize that increasing the overall communication competence of all employees and managers in organizations contributes to the quality of communication and thus to their satisfaction with it, all of which can improve the bottom line.

Conclusion

Our model of internal communication includes four key elements: a strategic management *function* responsible for guiding and steering organizational processes; a managerial *role* occupying the major part of any manager's work; functional *expertise* for improving internal communication policies, messaging, media, and relationships; as well as *participation* of members of an organization in internal communication processes, according to their organizational communication competence, in order to improve organizational processes and outcomes (Figure 10.1). The model provides a framework for description and analysis of internal communication and a heuristic to guide further study of internal communication in contemporary organizations.

References

Barnard, C. (1938/1956). *The function of the executive*. Cambridge, MA: Harvard University Press.

Broom, G. M., & Smith, G. D. (1979). Testing practitioner's impact on clients. *Public Relations Review*, *123*(1), 37–56.

Cooper, C. L., & Jackson, S. E. (1997). Introduction. In C. I. Cooper, & S. E. Jackson (Eds.), *Creating tomorrow's organization: A handbook for future research in organizational behavior* (pp. 1–4). Chichester, UK: John Wiley & Sons.

Dozier, D. M., & Broom, G. (1995). Evolution of the manager role in public relations practice. *Journal of Public Relations Research*, *7*(1), 3–26.

Gulbrandsen, I. T., & Just, S. N. (2020). *Strategizing communication: Theory and practice* (2nd ed.). Frederiksberg, DK: Samfundslitteratur.

Hallahan, K., Holtzhausen, D., Ruler, B., van, Verčič, D., & Sriramesh, K. (2007). Defining strategic communication. *International Journal of Strategic Communication*, *1*(1), 3–35.

Heide, M., Simonsson, C., Nothhaft, H., Andersson, R., & Platen, S. (2018). *The communicative organization*. Swedish Association of Communication Professionals.

Helsby, N. (2002). *The rise of the internal communicator: A research report on the role of senior internal communication practitioners conducted in 37 major UK and US businesses*. Watson Helsby. Retrieved from https://www.watsonhelsby.co.uk/assets/files/The-Rise-of-the-Internal-Communicator.pdf

Kalla, H. K. (2005). Integrated internal communications: A multidisciplinary perspective. *Corporate Communications: An International Journal*, *10*, 302–314. https://doi.org/10.1108/13563280510630106

Lewin, K. (1943). Psychology and the process of group living. *Journal of Social Psychology*, *17*(1), 113–131.

Men, L. R. (2021). Evolving research and practice in internal communication. In L. J. Men, & A. Tkalac Verčič (Eds.), *Current trends and issues in internal communication: Theory and practice* (pp. 1–18). Palgrave Macmillan.

Men, R. L., & Bowen, S. A. (2017). *Excellence in internal communication management*. New York, NY: Business Expert Press.

Mintzberg, H. (1973). *The nature of managerial work*. New York: Longman.

Nelli, R. P. (2018). *Internal communication in Europe: Key success factors and managerial approaches*. Vita e Pansiero.

Ruler, B., & Verčič, D. (2005). Reflective communication management, future ways for public relations research. In P. J. Kalbfleisch (Ed.), *Communication yearbook 29* (pp. 239–273). Mahwah, NJ: Lawrence Erlbaum associates.

Schoenenborn, D., Kuhn, T. R., & Kärreman, D. (2019). The communicative constitution of organization, organizing, and organizationality. *Organizational Studies*, *40*(4), 475–496. https://doi.org/10.1177/0170840618782284

Tench, R., Verčič, D., Zerfass, A., Moreno, Á, & Verhoeven, P. (2017). *Communication excellence: How to develop, manage and lead exceptional communications*. Palgrave MacMillan.

Thompkins, P. K. (1987). Translating organizational theory: Symbolism over substance. In F. M. Jablin, L. L. Putnam, K. H. Roberts, & L. W. Porter (Eds.), *Handbook of organizational communication: An interdisciplinary perspective* (pp. 70–96). Newbury Park, CA: Sage.

Veltsos, J. R., & Hynes, G. E. (2022). *Managerial communication: Strategies and applications* (8th ed.). SAGE Publications.

Welch, M., & Jackson, P. R. (2007). Rethinking internal communication: A stakeholder approach. *Corporate Communications: An International Journal*, *12*(2), 177–198. https://doi.org/10.1108/13563280710744847

Zaumane, I., & Leščevica (2021). Functional responsibility for internal communication management and its integration in contemporary business. *International Journal of Organizational Analysis*. https://doi.org/10.1108/IJOA-06-2021-2822

Zerfass, A., Buhmann, A., Tench, R., Verčič, D., & Moreno, A. (2021). *European Communication monitor 2021. CommTech and digital infrastructure, videoconferencing, and future roles for communication professionals. Results of a survey in 46 countries*. EUPRERA/EACD.

Zerfass, A., Moreno, A., Tench, R., Verčič, D., & Verhoeven, P. (2009). *European communication monitor 2009. Trends in communication management and public relations – Results of a survey in 34 countries (Chart version)*. EUPRERA. Retrieved from www.communicationmonitor.eu

Zerfass, A., Verčič, D., Nothhaft, H., & Page Werder, K. (2018). Strategic communication: Defining the field and its contribution to research and practice. *International Journal of Strategic Communication*, *12*(4), 487–505. https://doi.org/10.1080/1553118X.2018.1493485

11 Digital transformation and organizational change

Digital transformation and the organizational changes that it involves may be the most important challenges that organizations face in the 21st century. Billions of dollars have been invested – and mostly squandered – in digital transformation initiatives. There seems to be a consensus among researchers and commentators that digital transformation processes have often failed because they have neglected the human element: digital transformation and organizational change are about people. As a result, internal communication plays a key role in their success or failure.

Understanding digital transformation

The notion of digital transformation has become so popular in management literature that tech commentators are starting to question whether it has become a meaningless buzzword (Hurst, 2020). Organizations were investing billions of dollars in digital transformation even before the global COVID-19 pandemic, which has accelerated the speed of digital change. In the US alone, businesses were estimated to have invested US$1.3 trillion in digital transformation initiatives in 2019, yet approximately 70% of those initiatives were not projected to achieve the desired outcomes (Zobell, 2018).

Within the context of information systems, Vial (2019) developed a conceptual definition of digital transformation by drawing on grounded theory and reviewing 282 publications. He defined it as "*a process that aims to improve an entity by triggering significant changes to its properties through combination of information, computing, communication, and connectivity technologies*" (p. 119; italics original). He developed a framework consisting of eight elements, which he emphasized in italics: "*digital technologies* create *disruptions* triggering *strategic response* from organizations that seek to alter their *value creation paths* while managing *structural changes* and *organizational barriers* that affect the *positive* and *negative outcomes of this process*" (p. 118).

Although Vial's framework focused on the context of information technology, we can adapt it to the context of internal communication.

DOI: 10.4324/9781003200109-11

Indeed, his framework deals with the "SMACIT" digital technologies of *social, mobile, analytics, cloud,* and *the internet of things.* All these technologies – with the possible exception of the internet of things – will be, or already are, drivers of internal communication. Even the internet of things will doubtless affect organizational structure and corresponding internal communication, though empirical research is currently lacking.

The internet in general, and social media in particular, has turned corporate communication on its head. Until the end of the 20th century, external and internal communications were usually well separated, and internal communication was often conducted by human resources departments. Now, the internet and social media have empowered organizational insiders (employees) to become major influencers. Already a decade ago, top communication professionals in Europe and the United States agreed that online communities and social networks are by far the most important social media tools (Zerfass et al., 2012). In 2013, the European Communication Monitor reported that professional communicators in Europe found employees who are active on social media to be the most relevant gatekeepers for their organizations – even more important than consumers, bloggers, and online community managers. Communication professionals also agreed that social media content changes employees' perceptions of their organizations (Zerfass et al., 2013).

In the first two decades of the 21st century, the European Communication Monitor documented two simultaneous trends: the rise of social media from occupying a niche in corporate communication to dominating at the top, and a convergence in the importance of various social media channels (Figure 11.1) (Zerfass et al., 2016). These two trends have occurred in internal and external communication. In fact, major social platforms that began as external to the workplace have developed specialized applications for internal communication, such as Basecamp, Slack, Workplace from Meta (originally Facebook), and LinkedIn.

In 2013, social media applications showed the greatest growth potential, with a 30% gap between importance and implementation (Zerfass et al., 2013), with most communicators in Europe already at that time remarking on its power to enable communication with internal and external stakeholders at any time (Zerfass et al., 2014). All social media applications for employees are optimized for mobile use, and they are often integrated with human resources and management information systems.

While digitalizing communication brings far-reaching benefits for those participating in it, it also facilitates analysis by those wishing to understand and optimize it. Digitalization makes analytics of internal communication processes faster, easier, and cheaper, and it allows the collection of new types of data, on a larger scale than ever before. Applying "big data" techniques to recognize patterns in the large amounts of data can help researchers understand how internal communication operates

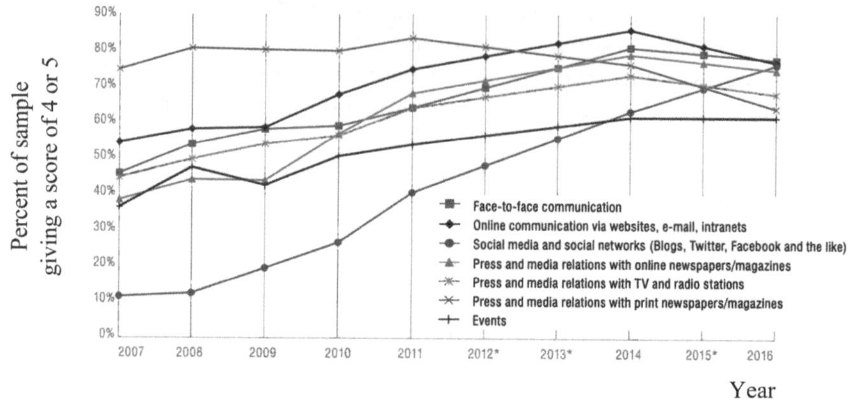

Figure 11.1 Relevance of key channels and instruments for corporate communication, 2007–2016. Data are from Zerfass et al. (2016) and are based on 13,709 responses from communication professionals in 43 European countries. The *y*-axis indicates the proportion of the sample indicating agreement of 4 or 5 for statements about how important the indicated channels are in addressing stakeholders, gatekeepers, and audiences today, on a scale from "1" ("not important") to "5" ("very important"). No data were collected in the years marked with an asterisk, for which results were interpolated.

in organizations and identify potential innovations and improvements. In parallel, the increasing delivery of computing services over the Internet ("cloud computing") offers flexibility and economy of scale for internal communication, whether at global organizations with employees scattered around the world, or at smaller organizations, who can now use software and data previously unavailable to them and who can access the data anywhere outside their headquarters.

Digital transformation and organizational change: the human element

Internal communication is intrinsically linked to change management. In fact, the European Communication Monitor describes a single discipline of "internal communication and change management" that assesses the importance of different disciplines in communication management of contemporary organizations and predicts their development in Europe. This combined discipline has been growing steadily since 2007 (Zerfass et al., 2007, 2011). The link between internal communication and corporate strategy is even more apparent in times of crises, when internal communication drives organizational change and restructuring. During the most recent financial crisis in 2007–2008, organizations rated the most important function of internal communication as supporting organizational change and restructuring (Zerfass et al., 2007, 2009).

The internet and social media have had a leveling effect on organizations, most of which are defined by hierarchies. The European Communication Monitor reported in 2012 that 82% of top communication professionals in Europe and 93% in the US were interacting with ever more stakeholders and more media (Zerfass et al., 2012).[1]

Today, internal communication is much more than just managing messages and communication channels. Van Ruler and Verčič (2005) proposed that communicators today also assume many other responsibilities, including training top management and other employees in communication. In fact, 74% of respondents in the European Communication Monitor in 2009 perceived communications training for managers as the most relevant future action in internal communication (Zerfass et al., 2009). Communicators are involved in aligning an organization's mission with the expectations of employees and other stakeholders. Van Ruler and Verčič (2005) named this type of communication "behavior-reflexive communication management".

The 2021 European Communication Monitor explored the roles that corporate and internal communicators perform in organizations. Based on extensive research on professional roles of communicators, the researchers defined the following five major roles, whose implementation in organizations they surveyed: the Advisor, Ambassador, Coach, Communicator, and Manager (see also Chapter 10). As communication departments grow, the Manager takes on traditional management activities of planning, organizing, executing, and evaluating communication in order to increase return on investment. In the 2021 Monitor survey of 1,141 communication professionals, 43% were performing the role of Communicator; 31%, Manager; 28%, Coach; 26%, Advisor; and 24%, Ambassador. These percentages indicate that the roles are not exclusive, making the job of professional communicator quite a versatile one (Zerfass et al., 2021).

Digital transformation and the corresponding organizational change increase organizational complexity and require ever more knowledge and skills in employees. This is another source of employee empowerment, which makes internal communication more demanding than it was in the 20th century. In the classical organization, there is a knowledge gap between management and subordinates, which allows management to command others and monitor their compliance. Formal communication is primarily vertical: orders come from the top, while reports come from the bottom. Such communication, however, compromises the performance of knowledge-based organizations of the 21st century and limits their transformative ability.

Good internal communication is essential for digital transformation because it is a crucial enabling factor in the development and acceptance of a common purpose, which organizations need in order to perform properly. In a start-up, the common purpose usually comes as a vision from the founder(s), but in larger and older organizations it must be developed constantly and recursively, in multilogue with external and internal environments. By bringing organizational change, digital transformations cause disruptions, uncertainty, and fear among employees and other critical stakeholders. In this way, internal communication is important for generating and cultivating trust inside organizations. In the model that we developed through the research project from which this book emerged (see Chapter 1), employees must perceive their organization as caring for them and thereby fulfilling the psychological contract, while also supporting them to be able to do what is expected of them, which should align with what they think is right. This explains why we found ICS to heavily determine employees' perception of psychological contract fulfillment and organizational support in our survey of 26 domestic and international companies in Croatia.

If we return to Vial's (2019) elements of digital transformation, we can see that digital technologies are triggers for processes intrinsically linked with, or even embedded in, internal communication. Disruptive digital technologies can have positive outcomes in organizations only if the perceived psychological contract fulfillment and perceived organizational support make the work environment psychologically safe enough to counterbalance the fear due to the disruptions, and only if the organizational environment features reflexivity through intensive internal and external communication.

Structural changes and organizational barriers are built up or torn down through communication or its absence. Successful digital transformation presupposes good internal communication and should contribute to it as well. Digital transformation is performed by and for people, and internal communication connects people inside organizations and helps them make sense of their work.

Digital transformation as a driver of hypercomplexity

Our societies are based on organizations, and formal organizations are the most important institutions of our time. The modern organization is based on the notion of rationality to make things effective and efficient, and on the division of labor. Rational organizations presuppose rational people being able to transfer objective information from those who have it to those who lack it. Generally, that means that information flows from the top, where decision-makers rationally plan, down to those who are hired to execute those plans. Large factories that use capital-intensive machinery, such as auto factories, are designed to organize production as rationally as possible in order to make ever more cars with ever fewer resources. Employees exist to follow orders, and horizontal communication between them is unnecessary and even irrational, as it diverts their attention from machines to other people. Internal communication has a very limited role in presenting the corporate purpose and vision; instead, it serves primarily to transmit commands from top to bottom, and to boost morale to make it all bearable. Employees usually remain with the same organization for their entire working life, naturally leading them to feel involved and engaged with their job and with the organization. The organization works to instill an ethic of compliance among its employees.

This modern organization is well suited to succeeding on the market when demand outstrips supply, when more railroads need to be built, and when cars sell faster than they can be produced. By the middle of the 20th century, however, an equilibrium was reached between production and consumption of many goods on the market, and overproduction has become a major concern. European and US corporations have faced growing competition from Asian conglomerates in the race to produce better products at lower prices, primarily through innovation and knowledge.

The postmodern era of the organization has created new challenges for management and employees. Competition and innovation are driving change, and jobs are losing stability and permanence. Innovation cannot be ordered and knowledge is hard to control. Given the difficulty of controlling knowledge workers, organizations demand from them an ethic of virtue.

Postmodern employees must be adjustable and flexible, moving within and between organizations. Involvement and engagement with the job and with the organization do not emerge naturally: they must be actively produced through strategic alignment between the organization and its employees and other stakeholders.

Internal communication has evolved in the postmodern organization to support these new challenges. In the second half of the 20th century, internal communication began to split off from other types of corporate communication, such as media relations or public affairs, to focus on employee engagement. Postmodern employees, many of them highly educated and qualified, must be "persuaded" and "seduced" in order for organizations to secure and maintain their mental, as well as physical, engagement. Internal communication grows beyond processes to develop messages and deliver them to the appropriate targets: it takes on the role of sense-making. It begins to drive, rather than merely follow, organizational strategy, with some internal communicators becoming valuable advisors and coaches to top and middle management.

Now, in the 21st century, postmodernity is giving way to an era that Lipovetsky (2005) called hypermodernity. This is a society in overdrive, characterized by hyperconsumption, hyperchange, and hyper-individualism. The flexibility and continuous change that began in postmodernity are accelerating. In addition, the transition from postmodernity to hypermodernity is not occurring smoothly; instead, the various trends overlap in a disordered fashion. These trends are being felt by 72% of European communicators and by many European organizations: while 14% of organizations are still "modern", 42% are transitioning from modern to postmodern, and 44% from postmodern to hypermodern (Verhoeven et al., 2018; Zerfass et al., 2017).

Qvortrup (2003) calls this society hypercomplex, with various forces transforming the modern division of labor into something much more differentiated and fragmented. The internet is creating the possibility of ever greater complexity, to which social media add further. On social media, we tend to segregate into like-minded communities to form "echo chambers" and "epistemic bubbles" (Magnani and Bertolotti, 2011), which affect how we see the world and create fertile ground for fake news and post-truth. These forces and processes threaten the unity of organizations and of society as a whole.

As one of its newly acquired postmodern functions, internal communication can integrate communities within and beyond the boundaries of formal organizations. To combat the overdifferentiation and disintegration of postmodern organizational life, internal communication can cultivate what Rose (2019) has called "synchronicity", in which members of an organization are synchronized – or aligned, as we described the same process in the previous chapter – with their environment. This requires the forging and maintenance of a strong organizational identity, which can emerge spontaneously but usually must be co-produced through interactions and relationships.

Digital transformation of internal communication

Internal communication helps drive digital transformation initiatives, even as it is altered by those initiatives. Too few communicators, however, seem to be aware of all the potential. In 2021, the European Communication Monitor found that communication professionals focus more on the technological aspects of communication than on transforming people and structures in organizations or on digitalizing organizational tasks (Zerfass et al., 2021). Similarly, the respondents in our survey of 26 domestic and multinational organizations in Croatia (see Chapter 2) reported that their focus was on reaching more individuals rather than on optimizing the message. As one interviewee said, "Digitalization is making it easier for us to get to more employees". This is a myopic view of digital transformation. Internal communication is already, or soon will be, experiencing significant changes going far beyond quantity, speed, and communication costs. Social media have empowered employees by making them important information gatekeepers, affecting both external and internal perceptions of organizations. This subverts the absolute information control that management can exert in traditional or modern organizations.

Another indication of the myopia of communication professionals is that only a fifth of communication managers in Europe saw innovation as a strategic issue for them in the 2007 European Communication Monitor

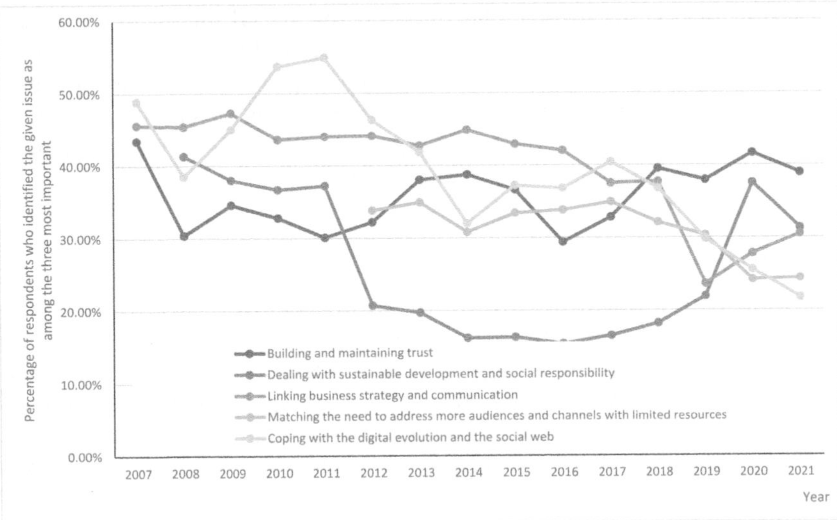

Figure 11.2 The five most important strategic issues for communication management, in the opinion of communication professionals. Data are from Zerfass et al. (2021). The y-axis indicates the percentage of respondents who identified the given issue as among the three most important.

(Zerfass et al., 2007). Since 2011, a declining percentage of communication practitioners see "coping with the digital evolution and the social web" as one of the five most important issues for the future of communication management and public relations (Figure 11.2). This contrasts with the fact that innovation is an extremely important topic for upper echelons of management.

These considerations suggest a lack of urgency among European communicators about digital transformation and the accompanying organizational changes. Digitalization is still perceived primarily as a set of new, fast tools, rather than as a transformative process. The impressive new technological possibilities are indeed a challenge for those who remain in an older mindset. As one of our interviewees said, "It is a big challenge to deal with new channels and the speed with which communication occurs today. This speed is on one side incredible, but on the other side there are at the same time many people who function as they used to 30 years ago. So, the problem is how to connect the two sides, equalize them and give everybody the same opportunities".

While adjusting to the speed and reach of new digital technologies is indeed a problem, we argue that the more urgent question is what qualitative disruptions social and mobile media will bring to internal communication. The traditional information division between management and workers is long gone, and the use of cloud computing and social media-based analytics is fundamentally changing the communication function in organizations. The internet and social media have democratized knowledge (Fuller, 2011), perhaps even "hyperdemocratized" it. In parallel, these new tools have made geography and time nearly meaningless (Scholte, 2008): regardless of where we are, we can communicate smoothly and instantaneously. The mediatization of everything includes internal communication (Tench et al., 2017).

Conclusion

Internal communication can occur automatically, like osmosis, from older to newer employees and from leaders to subordinates – but only as long as organizations change slowly or not at all. But this is not a viable option in today's hypermodern, hypercomplex world. As political, economic, social, and technological environments change with accelerating speed, so must organizations accelerate the transformation of their internal environments. Internal communication can support and accelerate this transformation and can integrate the resulting complexity into a coherent organizational identity and strategy. Modern organizations are characterized by division of labor, a stable work force, and rational organization; postmodern organizations, with emphasis on knowledge, information technology, and flexible workforce adjustments; and contemporary hypermodern organizations, with continuous change, decentralized information and communication technology (cloud computing), rapid workforce adjustment, and creativity. The defining characteristic of successful organizations in the second decade of the 21st century is digital transformation and organizational change, and these are human processes that must be suitably supported with effective internal communication.

Digital transformation brings disruptive change, which creates uncertainty and fear among employees and other stakeholders. Internal communication can take stock of the psychological contract between employees and their organization and provide support to fill in any gaps. Without effective internal communication, management cannot understand how employees think and feel, or whether employees understand their messaging and the underlying intentions. Even personal intervention by internal ambassadors may be needed. Digital transformation simply cannot succeed without employee support.

Even as internal communication supports digital transformation, it is being changed by that transformation. Social and mobile media, analytics, and cloud computing are redefining the role and demands of internal communication, which must become agile and inclusive. Digital transformation empowers employees by making them the most important gatekeepers for digital media for internal as well as external stakeholders.

As digital transformation accelerates organizational change, internal communication must reflexively and constantly innovate itself in order to remain relevant to management and employees as organizations become fluid and transform what they are, why and what they do, and how they do it. Strategic internal communication is needed to synchronize the various parts of increasingly hypercomplex organizations and society.

Note

1. In 2012, the European Communication Monitor coordinated its survey with a major US survey, the General Accepted Practices Study (Swerling et al., 2012).

References

Fuller, S. (2011). Can science survive its democratisation? *Logos & Episteme*, *2*(1), 21–32.

Hurst, A. (2020, April 27). Has 'digital transformation' become a meaningless buzzword? *Information Age*. https://www.information-age.com/has-digital-transformation-become-meaningless-buzzword-123489122/

Lipovetsky, G. (2005). Time against time: Or the hypermodern society. In L. Lipovetsky, & S. Charles (Eds.), *Hypermodern times* (pp. 29–71). Malden, MA: Polity Press.

Magnani, L., & Bertolotti, T. (2011). Cognitive bubbles and firewalls: Epistemic immunization and human reasoning. *Proceedings of the Annual Meeting of the Cognitive Science Society*, *33*(3), 3370–3375. Retrieved from https://escholarship.org/uc/item/60f049qw

Qvortrup, L. (2003). *The hypercomplex society*. New York: Peter Lag Publishers.

Rose, H. (2019). *Resonance: A sociology of our relationship to the world*. (Trans. J. C. Wagner). Polity Press.

Scholte, J. A. (2008). Defining globalization. *The World Economy*, *31*(1), 1471–1502.

Swerling, J., Thorson, K., & Renderich, B. (2012). *GAP VII: Seventh communication and public relations generally accepted practices study – Full report*. Los Angeles, CA: USC Annenberg School of Communication, Strategic Communication and Public Relations Center. Retrieved from www.annenberg.usc.edu/scprc

Tench, R., Verčič, D., Zerfass, A., Moreno, Á, & Verhoeven, P. (2017). *Communication excellence: How to develop, manage and lead exceptional communication*. Palgrave Macmillan.

Van Ruler, B., & Verčič, D. (2005). Reflective communication management: Future ways for public relations research. *Communication Yearbook*, *29*, 239–273.

Verhoeven, P., Zarfass, A., Verčič, D., Tench, R., & Moreno, Á. (2018). Public relations and the rise of hypermodern values: Exploring the profession in Europe. *Public Relations Review*, *44*, pp. 471–480. https://doi.org/10.1016/j.pubrev.2018.06.001

Vial, G. (2019). Understanding digital transformation: A review and a research agenda. *Journal of Strategic Information Systems*, *28*(2), 118–144. https://doi.org/10.1016/j.jsis.2019.01.003

Zerfass, A., Buhmann, A., Tench, R., Verčič, D., & Moreno, A. (2021). *European Communication Monitor 2021. CommTech and digital infrastructure, video-conferencing, and future roles for communication professionals. Results of a survey in 46 countries*. EUPRERA/EACD.

Zerfass, A., Moreno, Á, Tench, R., Verčič, D., & Verhoeven, P. (2009). *European Communication Monitor 2009. Trends in communication management and public relations – Results of a survey in 34 countries (Chart version)*. EUPRERA. Retrieved from www.communicationmonitor.eu

Zerfass, A., Moreno, Á, Tench, R., Verčič, D., & Verhoeven, P. (2013). *European Communication Monitor 2013. A changing landscape – Managing crises, digital communication and CEO positioning in Europe. Results of a survey in 43 countries.* EACD/EUPRERA. Retrieved from www.communicationmonitor.eu

Zerfass, A., Tench, R., Verčič, D., Verhoeven, P., & Moreno, Á. (2014). *European Communication Monitor 2014. Excellence in strategic communication – Key issues, leadership, gender and Mobile media. Results of an empirical survey in 42 countries*. EACD/EUPRERA. Retrieved from www.communicationmonitor.eu

Zerfass, A., Van Ruler, B., Rogojinaru, A., Verčič, D., & Hamrefors, S. (2007). *European Communication Monitor 2007. Trends in communication management and public relations – Results and implications*. EUPRERA. Retrieved from www.communicationmonitor.eu

Zerfass, A., Verčič, D., & Volk, S. C. (2017). Communication evaluation and measurement: Skills, practices and utilization in European organizations. *Corporate communications: An international journal*, *22*(1), 2–18. https://doi.org/10.1108/CCIJ-08-2016-0056

Zerfass, A., Verčič, D., Verhoeven, P., Moreno, Á, & Tench, R. (2012). *European Communication Monitor 2012. Challenges and competencies for strategic communication. Results of an empirical survey in 42 countries*. EACD/EUPRERA. Retrieved from www.communicationmonitor.eu

Zerfass, A., Verhoeven, P., Moreno, Á, Tench, R., & Verčič, D. (2016). *European Communication Monitor 2016. Exploring trends in big data, stakeholder engagement and strategic communication: Results of a survey in 43 countries*. EACD/EUPRERA.

Zerfass, A., Verhoeven, P., Tench, R., Moreno, Á, & Verčič, D. (2011). *European Communication Monitor 2011. Empirical insights into strategic communication in Europe. Results of an empirical survey in 43 countries*. EACD/EUPRERA. Retrieved from www.communicationmonitor.eu

Zobell, A. (2018, March 13). Why digital transformations fail: Closing the $900 billion hole in enterprise strategy. *Forbes*. https://www.forbes.com/sites/forbestechcouncil/2018/03/13/why-digital-transformations-fail-closing-the-900-billion-hole-in-enterprise-strategy/?sh=7d88aff27b8b

12 Internal communication redefined

Internal communication emerged as a multidisciplinary field of practice and research concerning communication in organizations in the context of management, human resources, marketing, and communication/public relations. It has changed from being from a merely supportive activity to a truly transdisciplinary phenomenon comprising a strategic organizational function, managerial role, professional expertise, and employee competence. The research from which this book emerged has shown that leading is communicating and that employee satisfaction with internal communication is an important predictor of organizational outcomes. Internal communication is the management of communication between an organization and its members in order to inform, motivate, engage, and co-create meanings, with the aim of making organizations more effective.

Studying internal communication

In our research project we studied 3,457 employees in 26 organizations in Croatia. Since we began collecting data before the COVID-19 pandemic and continued during it, we were able to examine how lockdowns and home office have altered internal communication. We based our empirical research on social exchange theory: we conceptualized internal communication as influencing social exchange between organizations and their employees. We confirmed that greater internal communication satisfaction leads employees to evaluate their relationship with organizations more favorably in terms of perceived organizational support and psychological contract fulfillment. Greater perceived organizational support and psychological contract fulfillment, in turn, strengthen employees' engagement and their perceptions of employer attractiveness.

In the organizations we studied in Croatia, internal communication was not a function on its own, but rather a daily responsibility of staff in corporate communication or human resources. Our results show that internal communication satisfaction is higher when organizations have a designated employee whose primary tasks include internal communication. Organizations where internal communication satisfaction is highest

DOI: 10.4324/9781003200109-12

feature at least one person whose job consists mostly of internal communication, as well as a CEO who has a positive attitude toward internal communication. This is in line with literature proposing that internal communication should be led from the top, meaning that it should be treated as a strategic management function. Managers should also view internal communication as an integral part of their role and activities. In the words of one of our interviewees: "Internal communication reflects the leader. In our case, internal communication drives external communication, because our external image is the result of what comes from inside our organization into our external environment".

The increasing size and complexity of contemporary organizations have helped drive the rise of internal communication as a set of practices and a field of research. We believe that this rise will continue to be driven by three processes. One is globalization and multiculturalization, which further complexifies organizations and necessitates greater concern for people within organizations. Another is digitalization and the integration of artificial intelligence into internal communication. A third is the hybridization and virtualization of work as much as possible, which the COVID-19 pandemic has accelerated. As a result of all these processes we expect internal communication to develop into a transdisciplinary field of practice and research, with its own identity within the organizations conducting it and within academia studying it.

Globalization and multiculturalization in internal communication

At the beginning of the 21st century, the world appeared to be globalizing ever faster, with people, goods, services, and capital flowing around the world. Then came the COVID-19 pandemic in late 2019, which led to the resurrection of borders and severely reduced travel and trade. In 2022, as the pandemic continued, Russia invaded Ukraine and thereby struck another blow to hopes for post-pandemic re-globalization. France and Germany began conversations about the need for European sovereignty to limit intercontinental interdependence.

These are only surface phenomena: behind it all, globalization continues to accelerate. Climate change has consequences for the entire planet, though it may affect populations to quite different extents. Declining soil fertility, water shortages, poverty, and military conflicts are driving people from their homes and making them global migrants. The internet is transforming the global "village" into a global "living room" – and there is no going back. Global movements of people and information are making organizations increasingly cross-national and cross-cultural.

Globalization and multiculturalization of organizations affect all elements of the internal communication model that we proposed in Chapter 10. At the top level, internal communication as a strategic organizational function must develop a vision of corporate positioning vis-à-vis environmental, social, and corporate governance principles, such as those articulated in the United Nations Global Compact for Sustainable Development (https://www.unglobalcompact.org). Globalization and multiculturalization raise ethical and pragmatic questions that organizations and their leaders need to address. Larry Fink (2022), the Chairman and CEO of one of the world's largest asset management firms, BlackRock, wrote to CEOs about "a new world of work" in which no "relationship has been changed more by the pandemic than the one between employers and employees … Workers demanding more from their employers is an essential feature of effective capitalism." He emphasized the importance of environmental, social, and corporate governance. Local success demands global perspective.

Globalization and multiculturalization also pose new challenges to managers as communicators. It will become more important for managers to be able to lead, manage, and listen to their multicultural workforce and to appreciate their diversity. Managers will need a deeper understanding of cultural characteristics and should develop an appreciation of others and their differences. Training in multiculturalism and sensitivity will be integrated into standard management education. Even if managers remain in the same geographical place for their entire career, they can expect to face people from diverse cultures and backgrounds. Once, it was necessary to travel in order to experience other cultures; now, cultures travel. All management is becoming multicultural management.

Globalization and multiculturalization also place demands on the professional expertise that specialists in internal communication need (Tkalac Verčič, 2019). Communication channels will be produced in more languages, and problems in intercultural translation will require experienced communicators who can detect problems at the earliest possible stage. Specialists in internal communication will need first-hand experience in working within different cultures, which means that they will need to show international mobility. These requirements will probably drive the development of a separate professional identity: internal communicators will be required to become intercultural interpreters.

Globalization and multiculturalization will be also become necessary competences for employees themselves, who will need to be effective at intercultural and multicultural communication in order to get their work done. Organizations will be required to train members in cooperation, mutual understanding, and appreciation of diversity, which will mean adding broader intellectual and practical dimensions to their work processes. There can be no internal communication in an organization unless all its members possess adequate communication competence, and this will become increasingly evident in the future. For that reason we believe that it is necessary to include all members of an organization, including management and employees, in the "internal communication equation": employees are subjects, not objects, of internal communication, the success of which depends on all members of the organization. Two-way communication can be accomplished only if both sides are willing and able to communicate. As organizations become more multicultural, their members will be required to be multiculturally literate and tolerant of other perspectives. Organizations that embrace multiculturalization will be better able to engage symbiotically with the increasingly multicultural environment.

Digitalization and artificial intelligence

One of the focuses of the research from which this book emerged was the channels of internal communication. While it is possible to communicate face-to-face in small groups, communicating across large organizations demands mediatization. This began with print and later came to embrace all traditional media, from print to radio and television, even including global corporate television networks. At the turn of the century, classical media were supplemented by the internet, electronic communication, and social media. Several of the interviewees in our research project commented that electronic communication was making their lives easier because of its reach and speed. But all added that no technology can ever completely replace interpersonal, face-to-face communication. As a result, "high tech" demands "high touch".

Internal communication is instrumental in digital transformation initiatives, while being itself affected by those initiatives. One of the new tools of internal communication that will be among the most challenging yet rewarding is artificial intelligence. The European Communication Monitor in 2019 and 2021 indicated slow adoption of artificial intelligence in the communication profession in general (Zerfass et al., 2019, 2021), and therefore presumably also in internal communication. We expect this adoption to accelerate and catalyze substantial improvements in internal communication. In fact, artificial intelligence will likely be complemented with augmented reality, which bridges the physical and digital worlds to make more information available in real time. This can benefit not only communication specialists, but all members of an organization.

Among the areas of internal communication that will be most affected by artificial intelligence may be its analysis and evaluation. Currently, most research in internal communication analyzes employee attitudes. Our work has shown that practitioners lack knowledge in research and evaluation, including how to perform communication audits in organizations and how to implement audit findings. Practitioners will need to upgrade their research competence. Artificial intelligence will allow for unprecedented, real-time collection of data on communication channel use, providing behavioral information to complement more traditional analysis of attitudes. What channels employees use, when and where they use them, what content they share, and what the outcomes of such communication are – analyzing these things may allow dramatic improvements in internal communication and render it much more quantifiable, similar to other strategic managerial functions. Better measurability of the "return" on internal communication may lead organizations to invest more in it. At the same time, such analysis may involve human manipulation beyond our current comprehension, raising important ethical questions. The adage says that "you can't manage what you can't measure", so richer analysis of internal communication may increase its manageability and improve its standing at the top management table.

Hybridization and virtualization of work

Digitalization has also helped drive the hybridization and virtualization of work and internal communication, which the COVID-19 pandemic has substantially accelerated. Hybridization and virtualization of work create new opportunities for organizations but also new challenges for managers, internal communication specialists and, in fact, all employees. The technology to bring together workers who are at home or in the office has been around for decades, yet its full potential has perhaps only become obvious to all during the pandemic.

We know from previous research that internal communication satisfaction is higher with rich media, which can be effective as a surrogate for face-to-face communication. Even as growing hybridization and virtualization of work move face-to-face communication to mediated communication online, our research during the pandemic shows that it is possible to increase communication satisfaction and thereby strengthen perceived organizational support and psychological contract. What matters is care, not physical presence.

Indeed, we found that the dimensions of internal communication satisfaction that improved the most during the pandemic in our sample of Croatian organizations were those that reflected direct effort by managers to communicate with their employees. Our comparison between before and during the pandemic illustrates how relatively small investments in internal communication can lead to substantial returns. Information and communication technology need not alienate people; when used properly, it can strengthen interpersonal involvement and organizational engagement.

Internal communication: from multidisciplinary to transdisciplinary research and practice

Internal communication is a practice "comprised of different strategies and tactics which all have a main goal of improving communication within an organization" (Tkalac Verčič, 2021, p. 247). Over the past century, it has been linked to several disciplines in academia and to several functions in organizations, beginning as part of general management, then moving to human resources, and finally to corporate communication and public relations. In a Delphi study, top academics and practitioners recognized the following disciplines as relevant for internal communication: management, corporate communication and public relations, human resources, psychology, language studies, media studies, and marketing (Tkalac Verčič et al., 2012). Each of these disciplines identifies its own problems and recommends its own solutions. Now, as organizations and their workforces evolve into globalized, multicultural operations in a post-pandemic world, the question arises whether internal communication can remain merely an object studied and steered by different disciplines, or whether it needs to emerge as a separate discipline and practice in its own right.

Alvargonzalez (2011) noted that "when human activities have a practical objective, the participation of a diverse set of scientific, technical, and technological disciplines is usually required" (p. 392). The growth in size and complexity of modern organizations creates challenges of communication and coordination, contributing to the emergence of internal communication as a discrete practical and theoretical problem. Social and organizational developments in the 20th century drove evolution of management theory and, within it, internal communication. Initially, communication in organizations was responsible for informing, educating and coordinating the workforce. Subsequently, such communication took on responsibilities of motivating and engaging. Today, the knowledge workers of contemporary organizations demand that internal communication allow them to co-create meaning in order to make organizations more effective.

This was the starting point for our definition of internal communication in Chapter 1: "Internal communication is the management of communication between an organization and its members to inform, motivate, engage, and co-create meaning to make organizations more effective". But how can internal communication achieve this, and what are the variables related to communication that we should measure along the way?

Our review of the literature and our research of Croatian organizations lead us to emphasize the performative nature of internal communication. Internal communication produces material results and changes physical nature. Higher satisfaction with internal communication leads to stronger perceptions of psychological contract fulfillment and perceived organizational support, which in turn reinforce employee engagement and employer attractiveness or employer brand. In this way, better internal communication produces better organizational outcomes. For this reason, we believe internal communication is an essential component of strategic management in contemporary organizations.

Internal communication is much more than a set of technical skills aimed at eliminating noise in channels linking management and employees, senders, and receivers. Employees are not passive recipients of messages targeted at them; for them to be productive and engaged, they must be appreciated as subjects in a two-way communication process. To be able to fully participate in organizational life, employees themselves must be able to communicate. Good internal communication depends as much on employees as it does on management.

Management cannot make full use of internal communication unless it considers such communication to be an important strategic management function responsible for contributing meaningfully to organizational success. The only way to get the best from employees and colleagues is to secure their active participation and willful support. This requires that managers understand the influence that good communication can have in an organization, and that they have the ability to communicate in an appropriate manner. Managers are, first and foremost, communicators: their authority is a function of communication, and they can achieve their objectives only through communication. Managing people means communicating with them.

In this context, specialists in internal communication are increasingly called upon to help managers understand and implement the strategic organizational function of internal communication, as well as nurture communication competence in all members of the organization. These specialists will need to draw on a growing body of knowledge (of which this book is a part), tools and techniques, and practices. Internal communication specialists are forming professional associations, and the subject is being taught at universities. Internal communication is developing its own identity and gaining a new position in organizations.

The time has come to recognize internal communication's independent contribution to the healthy life of modern organizations and their members. We do not communicate only among ourselves; we live *in* communication. Communication in formal organizations is different from communication in other settings. Our study has confirmed that investments in internal communication are investments in employees' attitudes that contribute to positive organizational outcomes and success.

Four components of internal communication need to be purposefully managed in order to exploit its full potential: strategic organizational function, managerial role, professional specialization, and employee communication competence. Organizations that recognize and nurture all four components will be winners in the future.

References

Alvargonzalez, D. (2011). Multidisciplinarity, interdisciplinarity, transdisciplinarity, and the sciences. *International Studies in the Philosophy of Science*, *25*(4), 387–403. https://doi.org/10.1080/02698595.2011.623366

Fink, L. (2022). *Larry Fink's 2022 letter to CEO's: The power of capitalism*. BlackRock. Retrieved from https://www.blackrock.com/corporate/investor-relations/larry-fink-ceo-letter

Tkalac Verčič, A. (2021). Closing thoughts and future directions. In L. J. Men, & A. Tkalac Verčič (Eds.), *Current trends and issues in internal communication: Theory and practice* (pp. 241–258). Palgrave Macmillan.

Tkalac Verčič, A. (2019). Internal communication with a global perspective. In K. Sriramesh & D. Verčič (Eds.), *The global public relations handbook: Theory, research, and practice* (3rd ed., pp. 195–204). Routledge.

Tkalac Verčič, A., Verčič, D., & Sriramesh, K. (2012). Internal communication: Definition, parameters, and the future. *Public Relations Review*, *38*(2), 223–230. https://doi.org/10.1016/j.pubrev.2011.12.019

Zerfass, A., Buhmann, A., Tench, R., Verčič, D., & Moreno, A. (2021). *European Communication Monitor 2021.CommTech and digital infrastructure, video-conferencing, and future roles for communication professional. Results of a survey in 46 countries*. Brussels: EUPRERA & EACD.

Zerfass, A., Verčič, D., Verhoeven, P., Moreno, A., & Tench, R. (2019). *European Communication Monitor 2019. Exploring trust in the profession, transparency, artificial intelligence and new content strategies. Results of a survey in 46 countries*. Brussels: EUPRERA & EACD.

Index

Note: Italicized and **bold** pages refer to figures and tables respectively, and page numbers followed by "n" refer to notes.

For Product Safety Concerns and Information please contact our EU representative GPSR@taylorandfrancis.com Taylor & Francis Verlag GmbH, Kaufingerstraße 24, 80331 München, Germany